"*Earthspirit: A Handbook for Nurturing an Ecological Christianity* is a gift to the church. For some time now, Christian theologians have been advancing new, ecologically sensitive visions for our time. The new cosmology of Thomas Berry is one of the most important. But often these ideas, including Berry's new cosmology, have been presented in ways inaccessible to the general reader. It has seemed to some that one must choose between 'the new cosmology' and a more traditional Christian faith.

"Michael Dowd points out that this choice is not necessary. He shows how the new cosmology undergirds and enriches traditional Christian views of sin, salvation, the Bible, heaven and hell, and Jesus Christ. He also shows how these traditional themes, understood in light of the new cosmology, can help us to be more open, rather than more closed, to other religions and to the insights of science. Can you think of a more important task for our age? I cannot. I recommend this book as a study guide for parishes and individual Christians who want to be open to the earth, to the cosmos, to other religions, to the human oppressed, and to Jesus Christ, all at the same time. We can thank Michael Dowd for writing it."

Jay B. McDaniel
Author of *Earth, Sky, Gods & Mortals*

"As one who is trying to live out of and educate people about the 'new cosmology,' I find *Earthspirit* makes an immense contribution, especially in its effort to dialogue with those Christians who love and treasure the Bible. Dowd grapples with key concepts of the biblical tradition in the light of a new consciousness about the human and the human enterprise within the 15-billion-year story of the universe. Dowd is breaking new ground thoughtfully and reverently. He describes *Earthspirit* as 'a handbook.' I suspect it will become just that with its helpful discussion questions at the end of each chapter, his many quotes, and excellent bibliography."

Jane Blewett, Director
Earthcommunity Center

"There has been little literature or religious support to make explicit connections between the 'New Story of the Universe' and the Judaeo-Christian tradition. 'Doing' this kind of theology has been experienced by ordinary, struggling people who are seized by a sudden revelation while washing the dishes, driving home, watching TV, coping with a fatal illness, returning to a childhood scene now covered by development.

"Questions of Torah, prophecy, prayer, Jesus, the beatitudes, or resurrection can suddenly explode within one's being. Drivers have pulled off the road shaken by a revelation that has echoes of Jeremiah. There are hot coals being pressed against many lips. Wavering hearts are translating scriptures into awkward scientific terms hardly recognizable to either the keepers of science or the keepers of religion. 'Ah, ah, ah,' they say. 'I do not know how to speak.' But speak they do and they are telling a story dreamed from the beginning of time.

"We are indebted to Michael Dowd for gathering so much of this insight and perspective into a form that is easily understood and shared. Weaving the threads of the New Cosmology faithfully and lovingly with the Judaeo-Christian traditions is a much needed contribution Michael brings to the worlds of scientific discovery and religious faith. This book is a most useful tool for women and men who cherish their tradition and want to open its meanings within the larger context of the evolutionary process. It opens the future to hope."

Miriam Therese MacGillis, O.P.
Genesis Farm

"Michael Dowd's book is a fine introduction to the 'new cosmology.' It puts us in touch with the thinking of many of the writers in this field. It also gives us a feeling for what it means to be in the 'habit of being the planet.' For those who see the need to begin living in a way that makes sense in view of the current planetary ecological crisis, this book serves as a valuable place to start."

Eleanor Rae, Ph.D., Director
The Center for Women, the Earth, and the Divine

MICHAEL DOWD

EARTHSPIRIT

A Handbook
for Nurturing
an Ecological Christianity

TWENTY-THIRD PUBLICATIONS
Mystic, Connecticut

Dedication

To Miriam Joy
born at home
the 17th day of July, 1990 A.D.
in Granville, Massachusetts

...and to her grandchildren.

Twenty-Third Publications
185 Willow Street
P.O. Box 180
Mystic, CT 06355
(203) 536-2611

ISBN 0-89622-479-1
Library of Congress Catalog Card No. 91-65198

Cover: "Earthrise in Human Consciousness" or "The Planet
Looks in the Mirror from 225,000 Miles"
(Photos courtesy of NASA)

Contents

ða 4 ða
What Does It Mean to Be Christian Today? 71

ða 5 ða
Transformed by Renewing Our Mind 79

ða 6 ða
Resources 103

Acknowledgments

Earthspirit: A Handbook for Nurturing an Ecological Christianity exists only because of the gifts and sacrifices of countless others—human and non-human. Thanks to the loving fire of our star, the sun, and to our most graceful dancing partner, the moon. Thanks to the sacred air, water, soil, and life of Earth. Thanks to Bash Bish Falls, which over the last several years has deepened my awareness of the living cosmos and empowered me anew when I most needed it. Thanks to the birds that sang so faithfully outside my window each morning as I worked on this book.

A special thanks to my mother and my father. Thanks to the members of the Granville Federated Church for teaching me about real ministry, and for their love, nurture, and support while I struggled to work out my theology. Thanks to the members of St. Paul's United Church of Christ for their warm, loving embrace of me and my family, and for their remarkably open-minded and open-hearted reception of the message that I have been called to preach.

Thanks to all who have formally and informally educated me through the years, especially the faculty and students of Evangel College, Eastern Baptist Theological Seminary, and Andover Newton Theological School. Thanks to Richard Clarke of the New England Institute for Neuro-Linguistic Programming for his teaching and example. Thanks to Tom Brown for his writings and excellent wilderness survival school. Thanks to Albert LaChance for introducing me to the prophetic truth of the new cosmology, and especially for helping me discover the transforming power of a twelve-step recovery program.

As will be evident to those who have either spent time with her or who are familiar with her audiotapes and videotapes, I am particularly indebted to Sr. Miriam Therese MacGillis. My work in many ways is but an extension of hers, with both of us building on the foundation laid by Pierre Teilhard de Chardin, Thomas Berry, and others. I thank her for teaching me how to communicate the new Genesis story and for her counsel and guidance. Thanks to Thomas Berry for his masterful synthesis of so many areas of thought, for his vision, and for his encouragement.

Thanks to Matthew Fox, Sallie McFague, Gil Bailie, and Gene and Joyce Marshall for showing me how profoundly relevant Christianity can be in our day. Thanks to McGregor Smith for his seemingly endless enthusiasm in promoting Earth literacy. Thanks to Andras and Deirdre Arthen and the EarthSpirit Community for reconnecting me to the ground of my being through ritual and celebration. Thanks to Lynn Margulis for allowing me to participate in her Gaia class at the University of Massachusetts, Amherst, and for inviting me to present the new cosmology to her graduate students. Thanks to Gary Beluzo for his outdoor companionship. Thanks to Elisabet Sahtouris for her wonderful telling of our evolutionary story, and for her encouragement.

A very special thanks to all my family and friends, too numerous to mention here, who add immeasurable value and meaning to my life. Thanks to John Briggs for inspiring me to buy a Mac Plus and write, and to Silvio Tavernise for tirelessly teaching me to use it. Thanks to those who critiqued the first draft of this work, especially Mike and Emily Patterson, who seemed determined to make a writer out of me in spite of myself. Thanks to Jill Tierney for her proofreading and her love. Thanks to Cindy Tavernise for her illustrations and enthusiasm, and to Steve and Michelle van Schouwen for their assistance throughout. A special thanks to my publisher, Neil Kluepfel, for his generous support and encouragement, and to John van Bemmel for helpful editorial assistance. Most of all, however, I thank my beloved wife, Alison, for her consistent love, support, and inspiration, and my children, Sheena, Shane, and Miriam, who playfully keep their father in the kingdom of heaven. Thank you, God, for all the above!

Introduction

There is a story told of an old monk who was visited in a dream by the risen Christ who suggested they go for a walk together. The monk, of course, excitedly agreed. After a long and contemplative stroll in the woods, the monk turned to Jesus and asked, "When you walked the hills of Palestine, you mentioned that one day you would come again in all your glory. Lord, it's been so long; when will you return for good?" After a few moments of silence the resurrected and living One said, "When my presence in nature all around you and my presence beneath the surface of your skin is as real to you as my presence right now, when this awareness becomes second-nature to you, *then* will I have returned for good." The monk pondered these words in his heart as they walked back to the hermitage in silence.

The next thing the monk knew he was awake in his bed. He was amazed at how real the dream had been. As he got out of bed, he noticed that his copy of the sacred scriptures, which he thought he remembered closing before retiring the night before, was open on the table. He picked it up and his eyes fell upon the story of the sheep and goats in the twenty-fifth chapter of St. Matthew's gospel. Moved to tears by reading this familiar story anew, the monk slowly walked outside in the predawn light. He crouched down before the still waters of a small pool in order to wash his face. For a brief but eternal moment he gazed at the reflection of himself, the trees, and the sky in the living waters. Just then he heard the whisper of a still small voice say, "You are my beloved son, in whom I am well pleased." The words of Christ in the dream came rushing back to him and he fell to his knees, kissing the rich, black soil.

☙ *The One you are looking for is the One who is looking.*
—St. Francis of Assisi

No matter where you turn nowadays there is talk of our global ecological crisis. Once the concern of only a handful of scientists and environmentalists, the relationship of humanity to the rest of the natural world is fast becoming the concern of all of us. Once reported only in little known publications, environmental and ecological issues are now being reported in mainstream publications with increasing regularity. Whether it be *National Geographic's* 100th anniversary commitment to spend the next 100 years working toward saving the planet from environmental destruction, *Time* magazine's "Endangered Planet of the Year" issue and follow-up articles, Meryl Streep telling us about "The Race to Save the Planet" on public television, or *Kiwanis* magazine's reporting on "The greening of the globe"— ecological concerns are being reported and discussed very widely and often. It is no longer uncommon to find oneself deluged with reports about the toxicity of our water, burned up over what is happening in the tropical rain forests, down in the dumps over our mounting garbage disposal problems, or blown away by the poor quality of our air. Global warming is a hot topic. "Green" thinking is here to stay.

Local communities are beginning to take action as well. Styrofoam cups are suddenly out, and recycling paper is in. More and more cities and towns are requiring separation of glass, paper, plastic, and disposable trash. People are learning to compost. On a larger scale, consumer pressure is beginning to force multi-national corporations into changing longstanding policies and practices that harm the environment. Whether tuna fishing techniques or fast food packaging, companies can no longer ignore the impact of business-as-usual on the natural world. And yet, even with all that is being said and done, many experts tell us that we are still on a crash course to a living hell on Earth unless the human family makes more significant changes in its thinking and behavior. As Lester R. Brown of the Worldwatch Institute reminds us, "We do not have generations, we only have years, in which to attempt to turn things around."

As a pastor I am often asked, What in the world is going on anyway? How did we get in this mess in the first place? What about our children and grandchildren? Is it really God's will that we destroy all the higher life forms of the planet? If it's not God's will, why are we allowing it to happen? What is keeping us paralyzed? Why doesn't the church have a prophetic word for our day? From our children's perspective, is there any realistic, this-world hope?

Everywhere I travel and speak to concerned church folk I hear cries ringing up to the heavens like the psalmist David's, "Where is the God of our salvation?"

Earthspirit grew out of my desire to communicate several deeply held convictions. The first and most important is that the God of our salvation, the same God revealed in the person of Jesus of Nazareth, is not silent, is not absent, and has not made a mistake. On the contrary, I am convinced that God is profoundly on the side of life, that it is God's will that the planet Earth and all its creatures live abundantly, and that the chaos we are only beginning to experience can be understood as a necessary passing of the old Adam in order that the new Adam might live. This is why ecological concerns necessarily go hand in hand with the Christian faith.

History will one day clearly show that we are at a major turning point, not merely of the human story but in the story of the entire universe. What follows is my attempt to sketch the contours of this transformation from within the context of traditional Christianity.

This book is divided into six chapters. In the first, I attempt to show how all meaning in life is derived from a people's cosmology, their creation/salvation story, and suggest that the main reason that we find ourselves in such ecological chaos is that we are, as cultural historian Thomas Berry notes, in between stories. We are out of touch with our true and larger Self. We have not understood and integrated the religious dimensions of the scientific story of the universe. In Chapter 1 we examine some of the more important features of this new scientific/spiritual creation story, what I will henceforth refer to as "the new cosmology."

In Chapter 2, we explore the nature and meaning of the gospel within the context of this new cosmology. I suggest that the scientific story of creation and evolution, told as a spiritual/ religious story as well as a physical story, not only does not contradict or conflict with traditional, biblical Christianity, but opens up some of its deeper meanings. I also propose that the process God used to create all things, evolution, is itself a revelation of God's will for creation, and that this understanding makes sense biblically, theologically, and scientifically.

The third chapter becomes more specific and examines a number of traditional theological and doctrinal catagories in light of the new cosmology. If the scientific story of creation and evolution is a revelation of the truth about the nature of reality, how does this affect the way we understand some of the core areas of our faith? Chapter 3 explores that question and points to the possibility that this new cosmology may even be linked to the long-awaited and hoped for "second coming of Christ."

Chapter 4 briefly examines what it means to be a Christian today, living in the tension of the "already and not yet" nature of the reign of God. After outlining an understanding of Christianity that I maintain is faithful to the Bible, tradition, and the new cosmology, I suggest that honestly acknowledging our pain and struggle and then wholly trusting in the unfolding will of God in the universe is our realistic basis for hope. This chapter concludes with a call to "disciplined love" for the sake of our grandchildren and all future life forms of planet Earth.

How we integrate the fundamental principles of this cosmology into our daily living is the subject of Chapter 5. After acknowledging that such integration takes practice and patience, I offer a variety of exercises and meditations/affirmations to assist the reader in developing the habit of seeing the world from the larger perspective that the new cosmology offers. The need to update one's internal imagery to fit with reality is then discussed, and the chapter concludes with a series of quotes from astronauts and others from different countries who offer insights regarding the human family's relationship to the wider community of life.

The last chapter offers an annotated list of resources for deepening one's knowledge of the new cosmology and its implications for Christian life and thought. Some of the references are also aimed at developing the skills needed to bring forth the ecological age, what has traditionally been anticipated as "God's kingdom, on Earth as it is in heaven." The annotated resource list is an integral part of the book, not an addendum but a chapter in its own right. Therefore, I urge even those persons who never bother looking at such lists to carefully examine this one.

Earthspirit concludes with a pledge of allegiance to Earth (page 119), which may be reproduced, modified, distributed, or otherwise used in any way the reader sees fit.

This book is designed to be used as a resource for personal or group study—something that can be returned to again and again. Questions for reflection and discussion have been included after each chapter to stimulate further thought. Each chapter contains quotes from a wide variety of authors that support or shed light on the topic. Some people find it helpful to take a quote and meditate on it in silence, as one would a biblical passage, being open to the leading of the Holy Spirit.

Several friends have wryly commented that I rely so heavily on the thoughts and quotes of others that it is not clear whether I should be listed as the author or the editor of this work. I accept that criticism. My purpose from the start was not to produce a major work of original thinking, but to make available for Christians as concise an introduction to the new cosmology as possible. Why? Because, as will become clear in the reading, I believe that the new cosmology can be understood as the good news (the gospel) of salvation for our age. Time will tell whether or not that belief is grounded in Reality. In the meantime, I earnestly welcome constructive criticism or honest feedback. May you be blessed, stretched, and deeply empowered by the new cosmology!

❧ 1 ❧

Cosmology:
The Foundation
of Meaning

We shall not cease from exploration
And the end of all our exploring
Will be to arrive where we started
And know the place for the first time.
                                        —T.S. Eliot

Where Do We Find the Meaning of Life?

❧ *Science without religion is lame. Religion without science is*
blind. —Albert Einstein

To understand the meaning of some thing or event—some
tragedy, for example—one must view it in terms of the bigger
picture, the broader perspective. This is how we must explore
the meaning of life, then, by examining its larger context: the
universe as a whole.

Anthropologists and cultural historians generally agree that
the largest possible context, the foundation of all meaning, is a
people's creation/salvation myth, or *cosmology:* their story of

how things came into being, how they came to be as they are, how the human fits into the scheme of things, and where everything is going. This story helps a people make sense of the mysteries of life and death, and is the bedrock upon which their religion, law, economics, medicine, education, and everything else is built. It embodies a shared set of unquestioned assumptions about life in a given culture. Like sunglasses with colored lenses, our cosmology colors everything we see. Not only are its rules and boundaries taken for granted; it is what we call "reality."

Anthropologist Margaret Mead once remarked that every culture she ever encountered had a creation myth. Every human society, on every continent, developed a unique story or set of stories that revealed the "truth," as the people gathered from observation and intuition, of the origin and nature of the world, why things are as they are, and the ultimate destiny of things. This story was their primary sacred story. It became their authoritative scripture when it was put into writing. As Christians, our cosmology has been the stories of creation in Genesis together with the gospel story of redemption in Christ. Traditionally, this cosmology has given our lives meaning and purpose, helped us to know our place and destiny in the cosmos, and given us a sense of right and wrong, good and bad.

  All professions, all work, all activity in the human world finds its essential meaning in the context of a people's cosmic story. —Brian Swimme

Biblical Cosmology

  Then God said, "Let us make humanity in our image, in our likeness, and let them have dominion over the fish of the sea and the birds of the air, and over the cattle, and over all the wild animals of the earth, and over all the creatures that move upon the

earth." So God created humanity in his own image, in the image of God he created them; male and female he created them. God blessed them and said to them, "Be fruitful and multiply, fill the earth and subdue it. Have dominion over the fish of the sea and over the birds of the air and over every living thing that moves upon the earth." —Genesis 1:26-28

It would be difficult to overstate the impact that the cosmology of the Bible has had on the thinking and institutions of Western society. A quick look at some of the traditional interpretations of the biblical story might help elucidate this.

From a straightforward reading of Genesis were developed the following beliefs: We were placed on a fixed, ready-made Earth over which we were to have dominion. We were made in the image of a God who was transcendent to creation. We were called to be in a spiritual relationship with God. This relationship was the only thing that ultimately mattered. Other living beings in nature were material, not spiritual—only humans had souls. Nature was in a corrupt state due to the fall of Adam and Eve. God would eventually restore creation to its original perfection at the end of time.

These beliefs form the presuppositional core of virtually every institution in the West. Whether we look at Western law, politics, commerce, medicine, or education, we will find very little that conflicts with this outlook on reality. These beliefs comprise the soil in which Western institutions have taken root, grown, and borne fruit. They have enabled and empowered us to make the discoveries and gains that we have.

For example, our belief that the world was material and that we were divinely mandated to have dominion over it is the reason that we were free to probe and explore nature, to discover how God created things. Because we saw ourselves as separate from and superior to the rest of the natural world, we had the detachment necessary for the empirical scientific tradition to progress as it did in the West. Our cosmology gave us the freedom to develop a wide variety of technologies, such as the telescope and microscope, enabling us to learn how the universe worked. It also inspired us, where we could, to reduce or fix some of the perceived imperfections in nature. The vision of helping to bring about the perfection that God would restore at the end of time has allured and empowered us. Indeed, the history of the West can be understood as a process of learning ever more about the natural world and developing technology to bring about less suffering and hardship, and more comfort, convenience, and longer life.

🍃 *A people's cosmology, or origin story, predates everything else that they create by way of culture, religion, economics, politics, and so on.* —Miriam MacGillis

Native American Cosmology

🍃 *Is not the sky a father, and the Earth a mother, and are not all living things with feet and roots their children?* —Black Elk

🍃 *The Lakota was a true naturalist—a lover of nature. He loved the earth, the attachment growing with age. The old people came literally to love the soil and sat or reclined on the ground with a feeling of being close to a mothering power....The Lakota was wise. He knew that man's heart away from nature becomes hard; he knew that lack of respect for growing, living things soon led to lack of respect for humans too. So he kept his youth close to its softening influence.*
—Chief Luther Standing Bear

🍃 *The earth does not belong to man; man belongs to the earth. This we know. All things are connected like the blood which unites one family. All things are connected. Whatever befalls the earth befalls the sons and daughters of the earth. Man does not weave the web of life, he is merely a strand in it. What he does to the web he does to himself. This earth is precious to God, and to harm the earth is to heap contempt upon its Creator....Our dead never forget this beautiful earth, for it is the mother of the red man. We are part of the earth and it is part of us.* —Chief Seattle

If we compare Native American cosmology with our biblical cosmology, we can see how it would have been impossible for the empirical, scientific tradition to develop among tribal people. Their beliefs would never have allowed it. In the creation myths of the native peoples of this continent the Creator was not seen as separate from or outside of creation. The Creator lived in the natural world and was present in and through all things. Since they experienced Earth as the Mother of all life, and matter as spiritual, they did not have the freedom that Western civilization had to probe the natural world and learn how things worked. There was no sense of detachment to make possible scientific exploration or technological development as we have come to understand them. And since God resided in the natural world and had ordered life the way it was, those things that Westerners experienced as evidence of "the Fall," such as suffering, pain, sickness, and death, the natives of this continent experienced as the necessary cycle of events ordained by the Great Spirit.

Different Cosmologies, Different Experiences

ꙮ *Our paradigms determine the way the world "shows up" for us. They determine our worldview, the way we perceive things, what we perceive, what we can see as possible, what we can't see as possible, and what we can't see at all.* —Werner Erhard

Pain and suffering were experienced quite differently by Europeans and Native Americans. Conflict over land is another example of different cosmologies leading to different experiences of reality. To the European, development meant remedying some of the perceived imperfections of this fallen world to make things better for human beings. To the Native American, it meant developing inner strengths like courage, bravery, and spiritual power. Given their cosmology, the Europeans easily and naturally thought in terms of *conquering* the wilderness, *using* natural resources, *owning* property, and *developing* land. The Native Americans, on the other hand, thought such practices were insane, sacrilegious, and ultimately suicidal. Why? Because their cosmology said that everything was connected like a sacred web, and that whatever we did to the land we did to ourselves. As Chief Seattle wrote to President Pierce in 1854, "How can you buy or sell the sky, the warmth of the land? This idea is strange to us. If we do not own the freshness of the air and the sparkle of the water, how can you buy them?"

At this point, we must be careful about making judgments about who was right or who was wrong. Such discussion is seldom fruitful. Neither cosmology is right or wrong, good or bad. We are merely describing how things evolved, and why Western and tribal people differ. This is not to say that every cosmology under the sun corresponds equally with reality. This is certainly not the case, as we shall see in the next section. What it does mean, however, is that every cosmology has evolved for a purpose, and that its purpose is usually only revealed over time.

Native Americans were not necessarily better or more ethical than their European counterparts; they just had a different cosmology. Different cosmologies naturally lead to differences in ethics and values. A people's creation story influences their experience of everything. As Thomas Berry has observed, "For peoples, generally, their story of the universe and the human role within the universe is their primary source of intelligibility and value. Only through this story of how the universe came to be in the beginning, and how it came to be as it is, does a person come to appreciate the meaning of life or to derive the psychic energy needed to deal effectively with those crisis moments that occur in the life of the individual and in the life of the society. Such a story...communicates the most sacred of mysteries...and not only interprets the past, it also guides and inspires our shaping of the future."

≈ *Do not judge, so that you may not be judged. For with the judgment you make you will be judged, and the measure you give will be the measure you get.* —Jesus (Matthew 7:1–2)

Our New, Evolutionary Cosmology

≈ *It's all a question of story. We are in trouble just now because we are in between stories. The Old Story—the account of how the world came to be and how we fit into it—sustained us for a long time. It shaped our emotional attitudes, provided us with life purpose, and energized action. It consecrated suffering, integrated knowledge, guided education. We awoke in the morning and knew where we were. We could answer the questions of our children. We could identify crime, punish transgressors. Everything was taken care of because the story was there. Today, however, our traditional story is no longer functioning properly, and we have not yet learned the New Story.* —Thomas Berry

≈ *Modern science can be seen as providing an account of creation that is the equal of any mythological, religious, or speculative philosophical account in terms of scale, grandeur, and richness of detail. More specifically, modern science is providing an increasingly detailed account of the physical and biologi-*

cal evolution of the universe that compels us to view reality as a
single unfolding process. —Warwick Fox

Thanks to our Western, biblical cosmology, we have made
enormous progress over the past few centuries in our understanding of how the universe works. With recent discoveries in
biology, geology, chemistry, physics, and astronomy, we have
come to see that the creation story that made our scientific
technology possible now no longer fits with what we have
learned using that very technology. Deeper meanings of the
biblical cosmology are now emerging. On the micro-scale, with
the splitting of the atom and explorations of "inner space,"
which scientists now say is nearly as vast as outer space, we
have come to see that all matter has a mysterious, psychic/
spiritual dimension.

Physicists are beginning to sound like mystics as they tell us
that every atom of the universe has an inner intelligence which
is non-material and ultimately unknowable (see Briggs and
Peat, Capra, Sagan, or Swimme in the list of resources). On the
macro-scale, as astronomers developed the ability to see and
hear out to the farthest reaches of the universe, they observed
that all the galaxies were rushing away from us, with those farthest away traveling fastest. Scientists were then able to use
this data as one of the ways of determining the age of the universe. They calculated the rate and direction of travel back-
wards and determined that everything must have emerged
from the same explosive center approximately 15 billion years
ago.

Thus, out of scientific knowledge made possible by a biblical
cosmology, we have learned that we were *not* placed on a
fixed, ready-made Earth. Rather, we are the latest evolutionary
development of an unbroken process of divine creativity that
began in a stupendous explosion of light and energy. Creation
was not something that happened once upon a time and then

stopped; it is something that is still happening. As evolution continues, God's creating continues! Since we humans have been given the gift of awareness and the responsibility of free choice, we co-creatively participate in the evolving creation of God as we give birth to truth, beauty, justice, and love.

A word should be said about evolution as God's method of creating. Though there is much lively debate over some of the details of the process, and unfathomable mystery yet to explore, there seems to be virtually unanimous agreement in the global scientific community that *some* form of evolutionary development is the process by which everything came and will come into being. As Harvard biologist Steven Jay Gould recently remarked, "The first thing that needs to be said about the theory of evolution is that it is no longer a theory; it is a fact. There may be widespread disagreement over some of the particulars, but that the universe has been evolving for billions of years is unquestioned by any respectable scientist in the world." Though it may be argued that this is an overstatement, it is probably not far from the truth. The biological, geological, chemical, physical, and astronomical evidence for evolution is compelling for anyone willing to explore the idea with a faithful heart and an open mind.

While the biblical cosmology remains religiously and mythologically true, its presuppositions about the nature of reality, as previously understood, are not literally true. Western science, which itself emerged out of a biblical cosmology, is now giving birth to a new creation story, a new cosmology! This is stupendous news when we remember that in all cultures, at all times, it was a people's cosmology that defined for them what was real and worthwhile, what was to be avoided and what was to be pursued. If it is true that our cosmology not only interprets our past but also guides and inspires our shaping of the future, then we are living at one of the most significant turning points in history, the dawn of an entirely new era.

❖ *Our most powerful story, equivalent in its way to a universal myth, is evolution.* —Lewis Thomas

❖ *What is at issue in scientifically framed debates about the evolution of the universe or the evolution of life is only the question of the mechanisms of evolution (i.e., the mechanisms that underlie the increasing differentiation of the universe over time), not the fact of evolution per se.* —Warwick Fox

❖ *The new cosmic story emerging into human awareness overwhelms all previous conceptions of the universe for the simple reason that it draws them all into its comprehensive fullness....Who can learn what this means and remain calm?* —Brian Swimme

The Shift in Perspective and Identity

❖ *The unleashed power of the atom has changed everything except our way of thinking. Thus we are drifting toward a catastrophe beyond comparison. We shall require a substantially new manner of thinking if humanity is to survive.* —Albert Einstein

❖ *The major problems in the world are the result of the differences between the way nature works and the way people think.* —Gregory Bateson

❖ *It is a peculiar fact that all the great astronomers of the 15th and 16th centuries were deeply convinced that the whole universe was a huge living being. Even during the height of western culture, the Greeks thought of the Living Planet organism as a fact of life.* —Eugene Kolisco

When we take the new cosmology as the fundamental context for understanding the meaning of life today, we see that the universe is not an object with life in it, as when we wonder whether or not there is other life *in* the universe; rather, the universe is a subject which is alive! It is an evolving, maturing, organism—a living system. The human is that being in whom the universe, after some 15 billion years, has reached such a degree of complexity that the universe is now able to consciously reflect on itself, its meaning, who it is, where it came from, and what it is made of. "The human person is the sum total of 15 billion years of unbroken evolution now thinking about itself," as Pierre Teilhard de Chardin noted a half century ago. The scientist looking through a telescope is literally the universe looking at itself. The child entranced by the immensity of the ocean is Earth enraptured by itself. The student learning biology is the planet consciously learning about how it has functioned unconsciously for billions of years. The worshipper singing praises to God is the universe celebrating the wonder of the divine Mystery whence it came and in which it exists. We humans are the means by which (or the place where) the universe can feel its stupendous beauty with conscious awareness. We are not separate beings *on* Earth so much as we are a mode of being or an expression *of* Earth.

Four and a half billion years ago the planet Earth was a great caldron of fire and chemical creativity. As Earth cooled, it formed a crust around its molten core, much like a film develops on pudding. The vapor from its boiling interior rose heavenward, cooled, and formed clouds. When the surface temperature dropped below the boiling point of water it rained for aeons, forming a planetary womb, the oceans. As the elements of Earth combined and recombined, becoming more and more complex, an inner spiritual development, a complexity of consciousness, was also occurring. Thus, when the complex structures that created amino acids joined together to form protein, Earth awakened into what we call life.

As the process continued, through greater and greater genetic complexity, Earth began to express itself *through* life in an increasing variety of ways. It developed the ability to breath through the respiration of its plants and animals; it learned to hear through the development of audio faculties in its creatures; it learned to see with the development of vision. Earth learned to heal, govern, educate, and nourish itself through its creatures, its living expressions. This continued until Earth had developed a brain and nervous system so complex and highly organized that it became capable of thinking about itself—and that's us! How each of us thinks is how Earth thinks, how the universe thinks in this solar system at this stage of its maturation.

It is important to note here that at no point in time during the past four and a half billion years, the age of our solar system, did anyone come from the outside and put anything on the planet. God is the *inner* dynamic guiding the process, the living reality revealed in and through creation. When Genesis 2:7 speaks anthropomorphically of God forming us from the dust of the ground and breathing into us the breath of life, that is a poetic or mythological way of describing the process I am outlining here.

This shift from seeing ourselves as separate beings placed on Earth to seeing ourselves as a conscious expression of Earth is, of course, a major shift in our understanding of who we are. It is a shift at the most basic possible level: our identity or sense of self. From this vantage point, we can see that Earth is not, as most of us Westerners have thought for the last several thousand years, a planet with life on it; rather, it is a living planet; it is alive. Indeed, scientists have discovered that over the last four and a half billion years Earth has maintained its average body temperature, while the sun's temperature has increased 25-30 percent. Earth has also maintained the salinity of its oceans and the chemical makeup of its atmosphere in a way that is only possible for a living system to do. This scientific understanding of Earth as a living entity is called the "Gaia theory," named after the ancient Greek goddess who symbolized Mother Earth. (See Lovelock, Margulis, Sahtouris, or Joseph in the resources.)

Beyond the scientific evidence, however, the fact that Earth is a living being just makes good, common sense. The physical structure of the planet—its core, mantle, and mountain ranges—acts as the skeleton or frame of its existence. The soil that covers its grasslands and forests is like a mammoth digestive system, into which all things are absorbed, broken down, and recycled. The oceans, waterways, and rain function as a circulatory system that provides life-giving blood, purifying and revitalizing the body. The vegetation of the planet, the algae, the plants, and the trees, provide its respiratory system, its lungs, constantly regenerating the entire atmosphere. The animal kingdom provides the lower functions of the nervous system, a finely tuned and diversified series of organisms that are sensitized to environmental change and have provided the first stages for the advent of humanity. Humanity itself can be understood as the capacity of the planet for conscious awareness or reflexive thought. That is, the human enables Earth to reflect on itself and on the divine Mystery out of which it has come and in which it exists. We allow nature, for the first time, to begin to appreciate its own staggering beauty and feel its own magnificent splendor. We humans are the means by which Earth has freedom, choice, and spiritual awareness.

Our planet and its creatures constitute a single self-regulating system that is in fact a great living being, or organism.
—Elisabet Sahtouris

The human is the being in whom the Earth has become spiritually aware, has awakened into consciousness, has become self-

aware and self-reflecting. In the human, the Earth begins to reflect on itself, its meaning, who it is. So in our deepest definition and its deepest subjectivity, humans are the Earth-conscious. —Miriam MacGillis

We are not at all used to thinking this way. For most of us, it is rather upsetting and humbling to do so. We don't quite know what to do with this way of thinking because it doesn't fit into any of our categories. For as long as we in the West can remember, we have thought of ourselves as separate from Earth and superior to the rest of nature. Our religious, economic, educational, scientific, and political institutions are all founded upon such thinking.

But we now have a radically new perspective on life. We have come to see that even though we are the means of Earth's self-awareness, we are also totally dependent upon the wider community of life, our larger body, for our own existence. In fact, we have no existence apart from living Earth. What we do to Earth we literally do to our Self. Moreover, we do not just believe this is the case; we know it in a rational, understandable way. (See Andruss, T. Berry, W. Berry, Briggs and Peat, Capra, Eiseley, W. Fox, Lovelock, Margulis and Sagan, Sahtouris, Swimme, Teilhard de Chardin, or Thompson in the resources.) This is humbling and disturbing news for Western humanity, and this is why faith is utterly indispensable in our day. Not "faith" that the beliefs we have grown up with are true in spite of evidence to the contrary, but faith that God is God, and that all truth is God's truth. We need faith like Abraham's, or Moses', who were willing to leave all that was familiar and trust that God would lead them in the direction of life for themselves and their descendants.

As in the days immediately following the discovery that the world was not flat and stationary, it will take quite some time before this cosmology becomes universally accepted, and before this shift in perspective transforms all our institutions. But that it will, eventually, seems as assured as that we would all eventually know that Earth was round and traveled around the sun—although most people five hundred years ago believed such a notion was absurd and heretical. As philosopher and psychologist William James observed about the history of ideas, "A new idea is first condemned as ridiculous, then dismissed as trivial, until finally it becomes what everybody knows."

It is true, however, that at the present time the vast majority of people in the Western world are operating out of assumptions of the old cosmology, and have not yet grasped the meaning and transforming significance of the new cosmology. As Thomas Berry says at the beginning of his recent book *The Dream of the Earth*, "One of the more remarkable achievements of the twentieth century is our ability to tell the story of the universe from empirical observation and with amazing insight into the sequence of transformations that has brought into being the earth, the living world, and the human community. There seems, however, to be little realization of just what this story means in terms of the larger interpretation of the human venture." Berry goes on to suggest that this last point is the major reason why our world is in such ecological chaos.

If a people's cosmology or creation story is their foundation for all meaning and value, and if our present chaos is due to the fact that we live and operate within institutions that are founded on a cosmology that does not correspond to reality, then learning this new cosmology and its meaning would certainly seem to be important for Christians to do. Moreover, if this cosmology is a revelation of God, if it is the truth about the nature of Reality, then not only will it not contradict the truth of Christianity, it will open up its deeper meanings and unleash its transforming, prophetic power.

⹓ *From the point of view of deep ecology, what is wrong with our culture is that it offers us an inaccurate description of the self. It depicts the personal self as existing in competition with and in opposition to nature.... [We thereby fail to realize that] if we destroy our environment, we are destroying what is in fact our larger self.* —Freya Matthews

⹓ *The greatest service the churches could render the world at this time is providing education concerning the facts of the environmental crisis, the ingredients in our current thinking and action that have contributed to the crisis, and the resources we already have available to us for altering our way of thinking and action in constructive ways.* —Douglas Bowman

⹓ *We cannot have peace on Earth unless we make peace with the Earth. This is going to require every sector of human society and it will particularly require the best organized sector of society, the church.* —David Brower

⹓ *The Earth is alive.... The Earth is a superorganism in the sense that it regulates itself much as the body does to maintain a constant temperature. The Earth keeps any number of environmental factors nearly constant, including a steady portion of a highly reactive gas—oxygen—in the atmosphere. Oxygen appeared two billion years ago when plants capable of photosynthesis first evolved. It was a deadly poison for the anaerobes (organisms that can function only in the absence of oxygen) that already lived on the planet, but the breath of life for the new organisms to follow.* —James Lovelock

Gaining an Evolutionary Time Perspective

⹓ *All the greatest and most important problems of life are fundamentally insoluble....They can never be solved, but only out-*

grown. This "outgrowing" requires a new level of conscious-ness. Some higher or wider interest appears, and through this broadening of outlook the insoluble problem loses its urgency. Problems in life are not solved logically on their own terms but fade when confronted with a new and stronger life urge.
—Carl Jung

᚛ *There is nothing in the whole world that is permanent. Everything flows onward; all things are brought into being with a changing nature. The ages themselves glide by in con-stant movement.* —Ovid

In order to gain any insight into the meaning of life in the 1990's from an ecological, Christian perspective, we must un-derstand ourselves within the largest historical context. If we imagine that our 15 billion year history was compressed into a single calendar year...the Milky Way galaxy self-organized in late February, our solar system emerged from the elemental stardust of an exploded supernova in early September, the planetary oceans formed in mid-September, Earth awakened into life in late September, sex was invented in late November, the dinosaurs lived for a few days in early December, flower-ing plants burst upon the scene with a dazzling array of color in mid-December, and the universe began reflecting conscious-ly in and through the human, with choice and free will, less than ten minutes before midnight on December 31!

Earth has not been thinking reflexively for long at all. We have only known that we were Earth thinking about itself for the last few seconds. We are destroying the conditions neces-sary for life in our preoccupation with "progress and develop-ment" (the supreme irony of our times), not because we are bad or evil, but because we are immature and ignorant of who we really are. Fortunately, as Miriam MacGillis suggests, "Earth seems to be coming out of its adolescent fixation with itself and its powers into a whole new level of maturity, and to the degree that you and I make that jump, Earth makes the jump."

The new cosmology is forcing us to make a number of significant shifts in our thinking. One of the most important of these is the shift from thinking that we could know the whole truth about something to an understanding that *everything* is evolving. It takes humility to accept the fact that truth, like everything else, is in process, and that time tends to unfold broader and deeper meanings of whatever is understood to be true. We used to think that those closest to an event were in the best position to know its meaning. We are coming to see that the opposite is more often the case.

The reason that time tends to reveal the deeper meaning of historical events is that it allows a number of different perspectives to emerge and shed their light on the subject. For example, we now have a far broader understanding of the "discovery of America" than Europeans in the 1500s did because we are beginning to respect the Native American experience. What was a discovery for Columbus was an invasion to them. The "meaning" of any event or experience is shaped by the perspective one holds. Berry comments, "When Columbus's mainsail appeared over the horizon in the east, every living creature on this continent might have shuddered... for everything that lives here is worse off since that fateful encounter."*

It must be remembered, of course, that the universe is still evolving. It is an illusion to think that we now know the *real* meaning of these or any events. Years from now historians will have a broader and deeper understanding of the coming of

---

*With this perspective in mind, especially in light of the atrocities committed by Columbus against the native inhabitants of this continent (see Sale, Turner, or Zinn), might it not be more appropriate, from a Christian stance, for the 500th anniversary of the Columbus's arrival, in October 1992, to be a time of sober reflection and humble apology to the Native Americans, rather than a time of celebration and prideful self-aggrandizement?

Western culture to the Americas than we do. They may even have insight as to why it had to happen as it did. The truth is that we can never know the whole truth. Time goes on. Everything changes in an evolving universe; nothing remains the same. This is precisely why faith—trust—is so important.

Literary critic Gil Bailie applies this awareness to our understanding of the gospel. He notes: "It was not those closest to the historical Jesus who first gave the gospel its geographical breadth and theological depth. It was Paul, who had never known him. In addition to that, impressive achievements in biblical scholarship have, in many ways, brought our era closer to the constituent events of the Christian movement than were, say, the Gentile Christians of the second century. If the life and death of Jesus is historically central, then people living a hundred thousand years from now will be in a better position to appreciate that than we are.

"Furthermore, when they look back they will surely think of us as 'early Christians,' living as we do a scant two millennia from the mysterious events in question. They will be right, for the Christian movement today is still in the elementary stages of working out for itself and for the world the implications of the gospel. There isn't the slightest doubt that the greatest and boldest credal assertions are in the future, not the past. It may be only at rare moments that this flawed and unlikely thing we call the 'church' even remotely resembles something worthy of its calling, but it is nonetheless embarked on a great Christological adventure. Even against its own institutional resistances, it is continually finding deeper and more disturbing implications to the Jesus-event."

☛ *What has been passing for Christianity during these nineteen centuries is merely a beginning, full of weaknesses and mistakes, not a full-grown Christianity springing from the spirit of Jesus.* —Albert Schweitzer

Questions for Reflection and Discussion

1. What were your favorite quotes in this chapter? Why?

2. What did you find most exciting in this chapter? Most challenging? Most insightful? Most disturbing? Why?

3. Was there anything in Chapter 1 about which you might say, "You know, at some level I think that I have always known this; I've just never thought about it like that or put it in those words"? If so, what was it? Do you suppose that this would be a common or an uncommon experience? Why?

4. What are some of the differences between mythological or poetic thinking about the process of creation and scientific or literal thinking about creation? Why are both necessary? Do you think there may be a corresponding relationship with dreamtime reality and daytime reality? If yes, how so? If no, why not?

5. Name as many ways as you can in which we are interconnected and interdependent with the natural world? How might this awareness broaden or deepen your understanding of the apostle Paul's metaphor of the body of Christ?

6. What might be some ways that you could practice being aware of Earth as your larger Self? How could you assist others in developing this awareness?

7. As this way of thinking becomes more and more habitual (experiencing yourself as a unique cell within the body of a living planet which is your larger Self), what effect do you think this might have on your everyday Christian life?

8. Similarly, as you develop the habit of seeing things from an evolutionary time perspective, what would be some of the fruit that you might expect to experience in your daily life and relationships?

9. Concerning the footnote about Columbus, what might be some ways that the church could witness prophetically to the wider culture around the issue of the Columbus quincentennial? At the national and international level? At the local level? What could you do yourself?

❧ 2 ❧

A Fresh Look
at the Gospel
and God's Will

❧ *All over the world this gospel is producing fruit and growing, just as it has been doing among you since the day you heard it and understood God's grace in all its truth.*
—Paul (Colossians 1:6)

A Natural Evolution of Christianity

❧ *People do not put new wine into old wineskins; if they do, the skins burst, the wine runs out, and the skins are lost. No, they put new wine into fresh skins and both are preserved.*
—Jesus (Matthew 9:17)

How may we understand our Christian faith in light of the new cosmology? How do we understand the meaning and direction of our individual lives within the body of the planet and the life of the universe as a whole? If the coming of Christ in Jesus of Nazareth was understood by Christians as a further revelation of the truth of Judaism, is it possible that the long-awaited "second coming of Christ" could have something to do with this new revelation of the truth? Although theologians will wrestle with questions like these for some time, I will point in the general direction where the answers may be found. The following reflections are suggestions for prayerful consideration and debate within the wider Christian community. They are offered with the awareness that time will prove them inadequate.

It may be said regarding the new cosmology, in light of the biblical foundations of our faith, that we are talking about a paradigm shift, not a competing philosophy. The new story of creation does not reject or replace biblical Christianity in any way. The traditional concepts of our faith are still valid, and nothing is being discarded. Everything is simply, yet importantly, being seen in a fresh way, as if putting on a new pair of sunglasses. The new cosmology may be understood as a further revelation of the gospel, not a different gospel. It is a broader and fuller understanding of the way things are and always have been.

From the Christian perspective, our faith was not a rejection of Judaism, but a revelation of the truth that could never have happened without Judaism. Likewise, the new scientific cosmology, which, as Berry notes, "seems destined to become the universal story taught to every child who receives formal education in the modern form anywhere in the world," is not a rejection of Judaism and Christianity. This creation story is the child of Judaism and Christianity!

The early Christians claimed that the truth of the Christian message was within Judaism all along, but that only in time could it blossom forth. The same may be said regarding the new cosmology and the biblical cosmology. This is why a growing number of theologians and scientists believe that this cosmology can be understood as an integral part of what the church has traditionally anticipated as the second coming of Christ. If this is true, it is good news indeed!

> *God has made known to us in all wisdom and insight the mystery of the divine will, according to the divine purpose which God set forth in Christ, as a plan for the fullness of time, to unite all things in Christ, things in heaven and things on earth.* —Paul (Ephesians 1:9–10)

The Bad News

> *If we do not stop and turn around, we will undoubtedly arrive where we are headed.* —Brian Patrick

> *We now know that human life depends ultimately on the continuation of other life.*
> —Peter Berg and Raymond Dasmann

> *We do not have generations, we only have years, in which to attempt to turn things around.* —Lester Brown

> *Do not be deceived; God is not mocked. You will reap what you sow.* —Paul (Galatians 6:7)

The term "gospel" literally means "good news." But good news is truly good only if it is understood as a saving response to specific bad news. The gospel has contemporary relevance only when it inspires faith, hope, and love in the face of the actual bad news of our present situation. For example, if my house is burning and I can't find my five-year-old son, there is no question what the bad news is. Now if, just as I am beginning to panic, my neighbor runs up to me and says excitedly,

"Your son just ran out the back door. He's safe by the big oak tree." I am going to experience that as very good news. But if I just discovered that my wife was in a serious car accident and is in critical condition in the hospital, and my neighbor runs up to me and says excitedly, "Your son just ran out the back door. He's safe by the big oak tree," I am probably going to think my neighbor is a little strange and ask him to leave me alone. I am not going to experience his statement as good news at all, but as irrelevant news. In the same way, a growing number of theologians, historians, and others are suggesting that one reason for the church's decline in numbers and cultural influence over the past hundred years or more in the West may be that it has been offering "good news" that has been perceived as irrelevant news by the wider culture.

The historic message of Christianity was true, is true, and will always be true. Yet we limit the meaning and significance of the gospel for all future generations if we interpret the "Christ-event"—the life, death, and resurrection of Jesus—as meaning only "the innocent lamb of God being slain as an atonement for our sins," to the exclusion of other interpretations. The reason this is so is because most people today do not believe that heaven is above them, that Earth is flat, stationary, and the center of the universe, and that hell is beneath them. That is no longer how reality is perceived. We don't live in a first-century world of patriarchal fathers and sons, kings, kingdoms, slaves, lords, lambs, sacrificial offerings, angels, and demons. This is not to deny the reality to which these symbols point. Reality has not changed so much as our perceptions and terms for it have. But if our children are to experience the gospel as good news, then we must interpret the Christian mysteries in light of bad news that they actually face. We must use language and concepts that they are familiar with and can accept as literally true. Otherwise, what was profoundly meaningful for past generations will either not interest present and future generations or will repel them, because it will not be grounded in the real world in which they live.

What is the bad news that confronts us and our children? Although a number of perils could be named, the threat to life itself would seem to be the worst news, both in terms of immediate impact and long-term consequences. The tragic fact is that all future generations of Earth-life may be condemned to a toxic hell because of our generation's addiction to consumerism and myopic obsession with "progress and development." It is bad news indeed for our children to see us paralyzed, unable or unwilling to make the changes necessary to keep them from this certain destruction. We will remain paralyzed as long as we think about ourselves and our world according to the old cosmology.

The fact that the entire universe is in process means that what was necessary or helpful at one stage of development might become problematic or harmful at a later stage. The conditions that were essential for planetary life to thrive two billion years ago, when there was very little oxygen in the atmosphere, would now destroy all the more complex life forms of the planet. Beliefs, too, can have a time when they are necessary and a later time when they are destructive.

The old cosmology is a case in point. We probably could not have achieved the scientific and technological breakthroughs we did without our having believed that God was transcendent, that we too were separate from and superior to the rest of nature, that Earth was a rest stop or testing arena on the way to our true home in heaven, that nature was imperfect and could be improved upon, and that the land was for us to own, use, and develop.

These beliefs made possible the revelation of the new cosmology. They allowed the knowledge of our true nature and identity to be discovered empirically. They served us well. But now we must let them go, for they have also brought us to the very brink of planetary suicide. In the long run, humanity will probably be able to appreciate how the brink we have arrived at was central to God's will. Presently our situation is perilous at best.

It is difficult for most of us to hear, much less to accept personal responsibility for the fact, that humanity is violently raping the Earth. We are cutting down rain forests, our own external lungs (which took several hundred million years to evolve), at the rate of one football field of forest every second. This is bad news for our children. We are losing over 18 billion tons of topsoil each year, and are quickly running out of usable farmland, thanks to our short-sighted, fast-buck methods of agriculture. This is bad news for our children. Our cars and factories are ruining the atmosphere, while our flush toilets and pesticides are ruining the groundwater. This is bad news for our children. We inject 82 billion tons of toxic waste every year into Earth's bloodstream, when already it has been estimated that 65 to 80 percent of all illnesses are environmentally caused or aggravated. This is bad news for our children.

Biologists estimate that we are causing the extinction of 20,000 plant and animal species every year—one species every thirty minutes!—through air, water, and soil pollution, and through our destruction of forests. These species, each a unique revelation of God, a face of the divine, and each necessary for the healthy functioning of the planetary body, took billions of years to evolve. Yet we are extinguishing them forever, without batting an eye. Why? So that we can live comfortable, convenient lifestyles, eat cheap beef, and drive to our shopping malls to buy things we mostly don't need. Surely, this is bad news for our children.

The list could go on: The growing hole in the ozone layer is bad news. The greenhouse effect is bad news. Radioactive wastes are bad news. And the ever-present possibility of nuclear war or accident is bad news. In summary, we and our children are faced with *much* bad news. But the World War that humans are waging against the natural world is by far the worst news. The irony, of course, is that if we "win," we lose. While planet Earth will surely survive in some capacity no matter what we do—bacteria and cockroaches are amazingly adaptive—its reflexive consciousness, the human species, may not.

In response to this bad news, does God offer any good news? If so, what is this gospel of salvation that we may joyfully announce to our children? What is God's message of realistic hope for the little ones who are faced with such bad news? If the promise of an eternity with Jesus in an otherworldly heaven with mansions and streets of gold is not generally considered good news by our children, if that vision of the future does not move them to faith, hope, and love, what will? The new cosmology seems to hold promise.

&♦ *The future belongs to those who give the next generation reasons to hope.* —Pierre Teilhard de Chardin

&♦ *Each of us must accept total responsibility for the earth's survival. We are the curators of life on earth, standing at the crossroads of time.* —Helen Caldicott

&♦ *To pollute, disfigure, or harm the gift that is the earth is to spit into the face of the Creator. But to take joy in the earth is to rejoice in God and to become like God, who takes joy in the creation.* —Douglas Bowman

&♦ *Unless we are totally depraved we will seek to give to our children not only life and education but a planet with pure air and bright waters and fruitful fields, a planet that can be lived on with grace and beauty and a touch of human and earthly tenderness.* —Thomas Berry

A thousand years ago, the civilized world faced the millennium with an almost frantic sense of foreboding. Religious leaders, having consulted biblical prophecy, had predicted that the end of the world was imminent. In the year 1000, they feared God's power would destroy the world. In the year 2000, the danger is that man's power will destroy the world—unless we take decisive action to prevent it. —Richard M. Nixon

Whether you believe that you can or you can't, you are right. —Henry Ford

The Root of Our Crisis: Sin or Cosmology?

Planet Earth is all that we have in common. It is impossible to damage, exploit, or care for each other more or differently than we do Earth. —Wendell Berry

A house divided against itself cannot stand. —Abraham Lincoln (echoing Jesus)

What is the root cause of our drive toward ecological suicide? Is human sinfulness to blame? Are we in the mess that we are because of gluttony, greed, and selfishness? Perhaps. These are certainly major factors. But if a people's cosmology is their primary way of judging right and wrong, good and evil, then the foremost reason that we are at war with our larger body is that we don't know the truth of who we are. That is, up until a few seconds ago (geological time) we did not even realize that the planet *was* our larger body. The vast majority of humans still do not realize this. An inadequate understanding of "self," not evil, seems to be the root of the problem. Sin is the fruit.

Virtually every Western institution—religious, social, political, economic, educational, etc.—assumes that we are separate from nature, have dominion over nature, and can use nature for whatever we want. Since this is the case, is it any wonder that we are where we are? Our present situation might be described as follows: Earth is alive and we are Earth's reflexive consciousness. But we have organized all our institutions and are using powerful technology based on the belief that Earth is not alive and that we are separate from it! That is the heart of the matter. The problem is essentially one of mistaken identity. Accurate self-identification is the solution. A couple of analogies may help.

The first comes out of the field of medicine. Researchers have shown that a cancer cell is a normal cell that has become disconnected from its genetic memory. Because it has lost its genetic guidance as to how to function properly, in cooperation and harmony with the rest of the body, it grows exponentially and ends up consuming the very body that supports it. Cancer always kills itself by consuming its own environment. This analogy is a good one, because it is addiction to our consuming (consumer) lifestyles that is killing the body of the planet.

Another analogy comes from research done on people with amnesia. For example, there was a gifted artist who was also a compassionate and highly resourceful woman. She was involved in a train accident in which she suffered a concussion and severe amnesia. For several months she had no sense of who she was, where she came from, where she was going, or of even whether her actions were appropriate or self-destructive. During this time she became fearful, distrusting, self-centered, and vulnerable to all sorts of illusions about who she was and what the meaning and direction of her life was. Ignorance of her past ruined her present and left her in despair about the future. Only when she recovered the memory of her true identity did she regain access to the resources she possessed, become reconciled to her family and friends, and regain a sense of her role in the community and a vision of her larger destiny.

These analogies serve as present-day parables of the cause and cure of our global sickness. Humanity has been suffering from amnesia, unaware of its true identity, cut off from its larger and deeper Self. Our hope lies in recovering our memory of who we are and always have been. As we recover, we will also discover how reconciliation to our larger Self and knowing our whole story open up the deeper meaning and potential of our Christian faith and empower us to transform our cultural institutions.

All human institutions, programs, policies, and decisions must be judged primarily by the extent to which they inhibit, ignore, or foster a mutually dependent human-earth relationship. —Thomas Berry

Do not be conformed to this age any longer, but be transformed by the renewing of your mind, so that you may be able to discern what is the will of God—what is good and acceptable and perfect. —Paul (Romans 12:2)

The Process of Evolution Revealing the Will of God

The Earth lies polluted under its inhabitants, for they have disobeyed the laws, violated the statutes, and broken the everlasting covenant. —Isaiah 24:5

If the whole universe emerges from the divine and is a revelation of God, then the prehuman process of evolution, on internal guidance or instinct, can be understood as having proceeded according to the laws of God. Thus, in order for humanity to be in accord with the will of God, it too must be in alignment with the basic laws of evolution. For if we are that part of the universe that has developed awareness and free will, then only as we are in harmony with the same laws that have guided the process from the beginning will we participate in this solar system's further evolution, rather than in its suicide.

This is not to suggest that our solar system is the only place where the universe is involved in this type of drama. There are well over 100,000,000,000 (100 billion) galaxies, each of which have nearly the same number of solar systems. It is quite possible, and perhaps even likely, that there are millions or even billions of other planets that are alive like Earth. We may be only one cell in the body of a universe with billions of other living cells. But we may also be the only cell in the universe that has evolved to the degree of reflexive consciousness. We don't know. What we do know, however, is that the further evolution or devolution of *this* solar system depends on whether or not the consciousness of Earth—humanity—freely chooses to work in harmony with the way the process has functioned unconsciously and instinctually for billions of years.

In the language of the Bible, we are being warned that if we and our children want to continue living, we must humble ourselves and obey God's commandments. Where do we find these commandments? Scientists have learned them most recently through empirical observation of the universe. But those with eyes to see and ears to hear will find them practically everywhere: in the law of Moses, in the voice of the prophets, in the life and teachings of Jesus, in the eightfold path of Buddhism, under a microscope, in the starry heavens, and within their own hearts.

 One of the scribes asked him, "Which commandment is the most important of all?" "The most important of all," Jesus answered, "is this: 'Hear, O Israel, the Lord our God, the Lord is One. You shall love the Lord your God with all your heart and with all your soul and with all your mind and with all your strength.' The second is this: You shall love your neighbor as

yourself.' There is no commandment greater than these."
—Mark 12:28–31

❊ *Who is our neighbor: the Samaritan? the outcast? the enemy? Yes, yes, of course. But it is also the whale, the dolphin and the rain forest. Our neighbor is the entire community of life, the entire universe. We must love it all as our self because in fact it is our Self. The universe is the primary subject.*
—Brian Patrick

❊ *Human nature is such that with sufficient all-sided maturity we cannot avoid "identifying" ourselves with all living beings, beautiful or ugly, big or small, sentient or not....Identification elicits intense empathy, so there must be identification in order for there to be compassion and, among humans, solidarity....Through broader identification, people may come to see their own interest served by environmental protection, through genuine self-love, love of a widened and deepened Self.*
—Arne Naess

❊ *One's real, most intimate self pervades the universe and all other beings. The mountains, the sea, and the stars are part of one's body.* —Willis Harmon

The Trinitarian Will of God

❊ *"The time is surely coming," says the Lord, "when I will make a new covenant with my people....It will not be like the covenant that I made with their ancestors. This is the covenant I will make," declares the Lord: "I will put my law in their minds and write it on their hearts. I will be their God, and they shall be my people. No longer shall they teach one another, or say to each other, 'Know the Lord,' for they shall all know me, from the least of them to the greatest," says the Lord. "For I will*

forgive their iniquity, and remember their sin no more."
—Jeremiah 31:31–34

❧ A thing is right when it tends to preserve the integrity, stability, and beauty of the life community. It is wrong when it tends to do otherwise. —Aldo Leopold

❧ We have not inherited the land from our ancestors; we are borrowing it from our children. —Unknown

Research in the natural sciences has uncovered a set of principles or laws that have apparently guided the process of evolution from the beginning. The names that have been given these principles are differentiation (or diversity), interiority/subjectivity (or personality), and communion (or interrelationship). As Berry says, "These three laws identify the reality, meaning, and direction in which the universe is going." They form an indivisible triune reality.

Differentiation (diversity) is that dynamic within the evolutionary process that leads to an increasing complexity and variety of expressions. From its beginnings in hydrogen to the unnumbered variety of species today, the universe has been coded to become increasingly more complex and differentiated. Evidence from biology, physics, and geophysiology suggests that the greater the variety of parts that make up an organism, the healthier that organism is. This seems to be as true on the macro-scale of galaxies as it is on the micro-scale of bacterial colonies. For example, the millions of organisms that make up their delicate ecological balance is what keeps the oceans alive and healthy. Extinguishing species in the food chain destroys the health of the planet as a whole. This is one of the most important reasons for humans to actively protect the diversity of planetary life. Diversity is what makes life work. It is what the

Creator delights in. The human is that being in whom the universe can contemplate and cherish its diversity, and give glory to the One who wills the difference. We are in harmony with this law when we celebrate diversity and difference. We are breaking it when we try to eradicate differences, as when we promote conformity or uniformity.

> *We must ensure the existence of the greatest possible diversity and variety of life on earth. We must challenge the right of nations, human institutions, and individuals to engage in activities which impair the long-term well-being of other human beings, other species, or the environments on which they all depend. —Raymond Dasmann*

> *A thing is right when it tends to preserve the characteristic diversity and stability of an ecosystem (or the biosphere). It is wrong when it tends otherwise. —James Heffernan*

Interiority/subjectivity (personality) is that principle which recognizes that every being of the universe possesses a unique identity and integrity since everything is a revelation of the divine. There is nothing in existence that does not have subjective experience, a personality. Everything in nature is a face of God. Every being, from individual atoms to individual persons to individual solar systems to individual galaxies, has a nonmaterial center, an inner intelligence. As MacGillis states, "Everything that is, is a truth, an unrepeatable expression, a 'word made flesh,' a temple of the holy." The human is that being in whom the universe can honor and appreciate all its diverse personalities, giving glory to God through reverencing the divinity of all things.

> *It is God whom human beings know in every creature.*
> —Hildegard of Bingen

Communion (interrelationship) is that principle which makes the universe a universe and not a pluriverse. Indeed, one definition of the universe could be, "the interrelationship of all diverse personalities." Creation as a whole functions as a living, maturing system. Just as every part of a living body is in communion with every other part, so everything in the universe is in communion with everything else in the universe. All that exists is interdependent and interrelated in an unbroken bond of communion. This bonding enhances and enables the principles of differentiation and interiority. The human, as the reflexive consciousness of creation, is that being in whom the universe can participate in the process through love. Love is the bonding of the whole through awareness and choice. To love as God in Christ loved us is to consciously celebrate diversity, reverence interiority, and enhance the communion of the whole.

‏ *I believe in the essential unity of humanity and, for that matter, all that lives. Therefore I believe that if one person gains spirituality, the whole world gains it, and if one person fails, the whole world fails to that extent.* —Mohandas Gandhi

‏ *While we have recognized the inseparable nature of the communion with God and with the human community, we have not yet realized that this communion, to be perfected, includes our communion with the earth. This is the unique awareness that begins to take place in our times. The body of Christ is ultimately the entire universe. Otherwise neither the incarnation nor the redemption is complete. Experience of this communion is so strengthening, so ecstatic, that it can provide the energies that we need to carry life on into the difficult future.*
—Thomas Berry

The parallels between these three laws of the universe and the traditional theological concept of the Trinity are more than superficial. This is another reason the new cosmology can be understood as a further revelation of biblical truth. Understood traditionally, the three persons of the Trinity are differentiated (Father, Son and Holy Spirit), have their own interiority (Creator, Redeemer, and Sustainer), and yet each is said to be in total communion with the other (not three but One).

Moses promised the Israelites that if they were obedient to God's commandments, God would dwell in their midst, guide them, and make them a blessing to all people. Jesus promised his followers that if they followed his command to love as he loved, God would dwell in them, live through them, and they would be his post-resurrection body. Today, a growing number of scientists and theologians are saying that we will realize our destiny only to the degree that we learn and live out of the knowledge of our true identity, surrender our human-centeredness, and come into harmony with these fundamental laws of nature. Or as Berry says, "The human community and the Earth community together form a single sacred community. We go into the future as a single sacred community, or we both perish in the desert."

Now what I am commanding you today is not too difficult for you or beyond your reach. No, the word is very near you; it is in your mouth and in your heart so you may obey it. See, I set before you today life and prosperity, death and destruction. For I command you today to love the Lord your God, to walk in God's ways, and to keep God's commands, decrees and laws. If you do this, then you will live and increase, and the Lord your God will bless you. This day I call heaven and earth as witnesses against you that I have set before you life and death, blessings and curses. Now choose life, so that you and your children may live. —Yahweh (Deuteronomy 30:11,14–19)

૨ॐ *The whole world and all creatures will be to you nothing else than an open book and a living Bible, in which you may study, without any previous instruction, the science of God and from which you may learn God's will.* —Sebastian Frank

૨ॐ *Our children need to learn gardening. The reasons for this reach deep into their mental and emotional as well as into their physical survival. Gardening is an active participation in the deepest mysteries of the universe.* —Thomas Berry

૨ॐ *Fundamental to all ethics is reverence for life: to protect and encourage life is good; to destroy and demean life is bad.* —Albert Schweitzer

૨ॐ *The Earth remains our mother as God is our father, and only the one who remains true to the mother will be placed by her in the arms of the father.* —Dietrich Bonhoeffer

૨ॐ *As we read, we move our eyes—and the whole interconnected universe moves.* —Joel Latner

Questions for Reflection and Discussion

1. What were your favorite quotes in this chapter? Why?

2. What did you find most exciting in this chapter? Most challenging? Most insightful? Most disturbing? Why?

3. Was there anything in Chapter 2 about which you might say, "At some level I think that I have always known this; I've just never thought about it like that or put it in those words"? If so, what was it?

4. What is the actual bad news that you face: personally? in your family? at work? in your community? as Earth? What would constitute good news for you at each of these levels of identity?

5. What are some of the major reasons why, both as individuals and as a society, we have failed to make the health and well-being of future generations our first priority?

6. Do you agree or disagree with the suggestion that the root of our crisis is primarily one of cosmology; that is, one of self-identification and self-awareness, rather than one of sinfulness? Why? Did you find the two analogies on page 37 helpful? Why or why not?

❧ 3 ❧

Doctrine in Light of the New Cosmology

❧ *Teach what is consistent with sound doctrine.* —Paul (Titus 2:1)

Different Expressions for Similar Realities

If we want to be empowered as Christ-centered and Christ-like agents of salvation in this world we must fulfill these conditions: 1) We must recognize who we are and develop habits that reflect this awareness. 2) We must remain rooted in our Judaeo-Christian heritage. 3) We must be mindful of the complexity and differentiation of language. While one person might preach about the need to repent, believe in the Lord Jesus Christ, and surrender to the will of God in order to enter the kingdom of heaven, another might proclaim the need to humbly expand our thinking and live according to the laws of nature so that evolution can continue with awareness. These two different expressions actually point to much the same reality. They bear similar fruit when followed. Keeping this in mind, let us look at how the new cosmology may reveal some of the deeper meaning of our Christian faith.

Sin

🙰 *Sin is cosmic treason.* —R.C. Sproul

If we are Earth at an evolved level of complexity and spiritual awareness, capable of conscious choice, then sin can be understood as any action or lack of action that goes against the revealed will of God, against the person of God. Something is sinful if it disregards or destroys diversity, violates interiority, or breaks down communion. To sin is to refuse to take responsibility for nurturing, loving, and befriending the body of creation or any of its constituent cells and organs. As theologian Sallie McFague has written, "Sin is the refusal to realize one's radical interdependence with all that lives: it is the desire to set oneself apart from all others as not needing them or being needed by them. Sin is the refusal to be the eyes, the consciousness, of the cosmos."

Sin means violating one of the three basic laws of nature. But doing nothing in the face of others who violate God's natural law is equally sinful. We are sinful when through either action or inaction we inhibit the development of a mutually enhancing human-Earth relationship. When we foster or promote such a relationship we are fulfilling the will of God, who is revealed in and through the universe. Creation is an embodiment of the divine. Thus, sin can be understood as an affront against a personal, living God.

🙰 *The recognition of sin is the beginning of salvation.*
—Anonymous

Salvation

🙰 *For God so loved the world (literally, "the cosmos") that he gave his only son...in order that the cosmos might be saved through him.* —John 3:16a,17b

ᴥ *Salvation is about healing, and just as the cosmos itself can be ruptured and torn apart by injustice, so too it can be healed by all human efforts to bring justice, which is balance, back to human relationships to earth, air, fire, water, and one another.*
—Matthew Fox

ᴥ *Both education and religion need to ground themselves within the story of the universe as we now understand this story through empirical knowledge. Within this functional cosmology we can overcome our alienation and begin the renewal of life on a sustainable basis. This story is a numinous, revelatory story that could evoke the vision and energy required to bring not only ourselves but the entire planet into a new order of magnificence.* —Thomas Berry

If every human being is like a conscious cell within the body of Earth, salvation may be understood at both personal and planetary levels. Personal salvation can be understood as a transformation that frees us from bondage to sinful and addictive patterns of thinking and behavior. It is the process of reconciling with God, other people, and nature—with one's larger Self—and participating in the reign of love and truth. To be "saved" or "born again" is to be realigned with the will of God, to be reconnected to the life of the body, and to be freed to participate in the further development of the universe through love. It is to realize one's intimate connection to the divine, that each of us is a revelation of God, and to walk humbly, responsibly, and obediently in the light of this grace.

For Christians, Jesus Christ is the prime example of how to do this. His life and teachings reveal the way to personal salvation and participation in the reign of God: unconditional, self-expansive love.

If the first level of salvation is realignment of the individual cell with the will of the larger body of the universe, the second level can be understood as the salvation of the body itself: in our case the living planet of which we are an integral part. Given the new cosmology, it makes little sense to be committed to personal salvation unless one is equally committed to Earth's salvation. If a physical body dies, all the cells of that body die with it. Likewise, if Earth is lost, the entire human species is lost with it.

Although the old cosmology implied that we had an existence apart from Earth, we now understand that we are the means by which Earth has recently developed self-reflective awareness. Thus, personal and global salvation are two dimensions of the same divine process. This finds support in the Bible: Jesus died to save the entire cosmos, not merely a select group of human beings.

> 🕮 *For in Christ all the fullness of God was pleased to dwell, and through him God was pleased to reconcile to himself all things, whether on earth or in heaven, by making peace through his blood, shed on the cross.* —Paul (Colossians 1:19–20)

> 🕮 *Whence can a human body have received its soul, if the body of the world does not possess a soul?* —Plato

We humans are the newest and riskiest development of the universe. If we recall our cosmological time-line, this solar system has only had awareness and choice for the last ten minutes of the year, and has only known that was the case for the last few seconds! It is important, then, that we remember: sin is the fruit, not the root, of the problem. Sin is the result, not the cause. The root of the problem is alienation from our larger Self, or, we could say, too narrowly defining our sense of self. We have been acting sinfully because, like a cancer cell disconnected from its genetic guidance, or like a person suffering from amnesia, we have not known our true identity and have not had access to the resources of our larger Self. Salvation is being reconnected to our genetic heritage, recovering our memory, and coming home, like the prodigal son, to loving, forgiving arms.

Salvation, whether personal or planetary, is a gracious gift of God. But it is also participatory. We are integral to the process. Only as we respond to God's grace with evangelical commitment and integrity, together with humility, responsibility, and obedience, will we be effective agents of God's salvation of the world. Jesus didn't do it all for us; he showed us the only way to do it. There is a world of difference between the two. Christ-likeness is the way of salvation, personally or "planetarily."

> *Jesus called the crowd with his disciples, and said to everyone, "If any want to become my followers, let them deny themselves and take up their cross and follow me. For those who want to save their life will lose it, and those who lose their life for the sake of the gospel, will save it."* —Mark 8:34-35

> *Every individual on the planet must be made aware of its vulnerability and of the urgent need to preserve it. No attempt to protect the environment will be successful in the long run unless ordinary people...are willing to adjust their lifestyles. Our wasteful, careless ways must become a thing of the past. We must recycle more, procreate less, turn off lights, use mass transit, do a thousand things differently in our everyday lives. We owe this not only to ourselves and our children but also to the unborn generations who will one day inherit the earth.*
> —Time (January 2, 1989)

> *Never doubt that a small group of thoughtful, committed citizens can change the world. Indeed, it is the only thing that ever has.* —Margaret Mead

🕊 *All things are possible once enough human beings realize that everything is at stake.* —Norman Cousins

🕊 *See, now is the acceptable time, now is the day of salvation!* —Paul (2 Corinthians 6:2)

Evangelism

🕊 *Go therefore and make disciples of all nations...teaching them to obey everything I have commanded you. And be assured, I am with you always, to the end of time.*
—Jesus (Matthew 28:19–20)

How can we understand the call to "evangelize the world," given the nature of sin and salvation as outlined above? Well, if evangelism means to proclaim the good news of salvation in word and deed, then the primary evangelistic task of our age would seem to be telling the story of the universe in its spiritual integrity. Teaching the new cosmology around the world will be the first order of business for evangelism in the third millennium. Of course, our lives and lifestyles must be consistent with the message we proclaim in order to accomplish this task faithfully.

Telling the new story of creation is essential because as long as the most powerful and influential humans are operating with outdated beliefs about who they are and what the nature of reality is, global salvation is virtually impossible. Evidence suggests that we will remain an uncontrollable cancer in the body of Earth as long as we believe that we are separate from and superior to the rest of nature, that God is transcendent and outside the process, that Earth is only a material resource, or that these are the "end times." The only hope our grandchildren seem to have of being saved from a living hell on Earth is our making the shift in awareness, and basing our ethics and institutions on the fundamental laws of the universe: differentiation, interiority, and communion. We need a species-wide "renewing of our mind" (Romans 12:2).

The late Gregory Bateson was a philosopher, biologist, and psychologist with strong Christian convictions. He knew well the difference between the old and new cosmologies and the importance of aligning our thinking with the true nature of things. He wrote, "If you put God outside and set him vis-a-vis his creation, and you have the idea that you are created in God's image, you will logically and naturally see yourself as outside and against the things around you. And as you unrightfully claim all mind to yourself, you will see the world around you as mindless, and therefore not entitled to moral or ethical consideration. The environment will seem to be yours to exploit. Your survival unit will be you and your folks against the environment of other social units, other races, and the brutes and vegetables. If this is your estimate of your relation to nature and you have an advanced technology, your likelihood of survival will be that of a snowball in hell. You will die either of the toxic by-products of your own hate, or simply of overpopulation and overgrazing."

* *Good people are dangerous when they are operating out of assumptions about reality which do not in fact correspond to reality.* —Thomas Berry

To "evangelize the world" or "preach the gospel" in the coming millennium will mean educating people in the new cosmology from a Christian perspective. The modern evangelist becomes a new storyteller: recounting the revelational tale of creation and salvation from its fiery beginnings, through the evolution of life, the various cultural and religious periods, through the life, teachings, death, and resurrection of Jesus Christ, through the development of Christianity and the rise of the scientific-technological world, to the realistic vision of the emerging ecological age. Physicist Brian Swimme recently exclaimed, "Our situation is similar to that of the early Christians. They had nothing—nothing but a profound revelatory experience. They did nothing—nothing but wander about telling a new story. Yet the Western world entered a transformation from which it has never recovered." If the salvation of all future generations depends in large part on our living and telling our larger Story, is this not an evangelistic mandate?

> *The most urgent religious task of our age is to help humanity become aware of its true nature and destiny. It is to preach the gospel in such a way that people come to know themselves as the reflective consciousness of the living Earth, and come to live with Christ-like identity, integrity and love out of that knowledge.* —Brian Patrick

The Bible

> *Ask the animals, and they shall teach you; the birds of the air, and they shall instruct you. Speak to the Earth and it shall teach you.* —Job 12:7-8

> *Every creature is a word of God and is a book about God.* —Meister Eckhart

> *You search the scriptures because you think that in them you have eternal life; and it is they that testify on my behalf. Yet you refuse to come to me to have life.* —Jesus (John 5:39–40)

How can we understand the place and authority of the scriptures in light of the new cosmology, the New Story? To answer this we can look to the earliest followers of Jesus as our example. In first-century Palestine, the only authoritative scriptures were the Hebrew scriptures, what Christians eventually came to know as the Old Testament. As the apostles and their followers became convinced that the life, death, and resurrection of Jesus was a genuine revelation of God, they went back to their scriptures with a new perspective. They saw deeper meaning in familiar passages. New insights into old problems emerged. All of reality was experienced differently by them in light of the revelation that God was in Christ Jesus.

After telling stories about Jesus for a number of years, some of his followers began to write them down. Letters, too, were written. Some of these stories and letters were collected and became what we know as the New Testament. For the early Christians, the New Testament did not replace the Hebrew scriptures. Their experience was that the New Testament built on and opened up the deeper meaning of the Hebrew scriptures. It would have been impossible for Christians to have the New Testament without the Old Testament. Such is the case today with the new and the old cosmologies.

The new cosmology is a revelation of God's saving grace, a creation story that is literally as well as religiously true. Though the old cosmology is arguably responsible for much of the ecological devastation that is occurring, it is also true that we could not have come to the revelation of who we are without going through this stage of development. Thus, if the biblical story contributed to the crisis, it has also provided the solution. Years from now it will be much clearer why we had to come down this road. We can trust that someday it will all be seen as unfolding the will of God. So the truth and importance of the written Word of God is not in question here. The Bible has been, is now, and always will be our inspired and authoritative spiritual guide. We are seriously out of step with the Holy Spirit today, though, if we continue to read the Bible through the lenses of the old cosmology. This is not only due to the danger of failing to respect and care for the whole of creation inherent in the old way of seeing, but also because to do so essentially limits God's communication and revelation to that understanding given two thousand years ago.

If the Bible's life-giving and life-saving message is to be heard in a life-changing way today, we must read it from the perspective of the reality of who we are, where we came from, and where we are going. We would do well to remember, though, that each biblical author necessarily looked at the universe through the lenses of the old cosmology. No person living before this century could know this cosmology in the way we now know it. The tools of scientific observation had not evolved to the degree that would have been necessary for such a revelation to occur. But the new cosmology did not develop in a vacuum either. We probably would never have come to this truth about God, ourselves, and the living cosmos of which we are an integral part without the foundation laid by the Bible.

The Bible is sacred scripture for Christians. The new cosmology affirms this fact and opens up fresh insights as to how it may be understood. The new creation story simply goes on to recognize that our primary sacred scripture, the first place we meet the divine, is the natural world itself. Nature is the primary Bible. Without the natural world there would be no written scriptures. The prior revelation of air, water, soil, and life made possible the paper, ink, and human consciousness that brought the Bible into existence. This is not a trivialization of the written Word of God. It simply recognizes and honors the living Word of God, which includes Jesus, as primary.

❧ *The universe is the primary revelation of the divine, the primary scripture, the primary locus of divine-human communion.* —Thomas Berry

❧ *Never does Nature say one thing and Wisdom another.* —Juvenal

Other Religions

⁋ *I have other sheep that do not belong to this fold. I must bring them also. They too will listen to my voice, and there shall be one flock and one shepherd.* —Jesus (John 10:16)

⁋ *May they be one, Father, as we are one.* —Jesus (John 17:22)

If the human is how the planet Earth looks out at the universe and thinks about itself and the larger body of which it is a part, and if life is differentiated by design, then people living in different places would naturally develop different ways of relating to God and the mysteries of life and death. The experiences of people living in the Himalayan mountains differ greatly from those living in central Africa. Lambs may be economically and religiously meaningful in the Near East, but they are utterly meaningless in the Alaskan tundra. Each culture developed its creation story based on its experience of the world and an inner, intuitive sense of knowing. Since a people's religion develops within the context of their existing cosmology, different people around the world developed different religious systems, forms of worship, and ways of coming into contact with the divine.

From the larger perspective, we could say that Earth has been evolving in its spiritual life differently all over the world. It has grown its spiritual branches differently in different places. The various religions are differentiated ways that Earth has learned to relate to that mysterious Reality that some traditions call God. And the crucial thing for us to remember is that God wills the differences! Diversity is part of the very essence of the universe; it is one of God's unbreakable laws. It should not surprise us, then, nor threaten us, that in spite of all our missionary endeavors, most of the peoples of the world have not converted to Christianity.

Even though it is a humbling truth for some of us to accept, the primary scriptures of the natural world clearly indicate that God's will never was, is not now, and never will be that everyone convert to Christianity. This would violate the revealed will of God, the three basic laws of evolution. That is why it is so important that we understand our written scripture in the context of the primary scripture. Each tradition, no matter how differentiated from ours, is a unique expression of Earth's spiritual life and has its own special gifts to bring to the larger body. We responsibly participate in the further evolution of the universe only as we are both humble and faithful, being as willing to listen and learn as we are to share our truth. This does not mean that everything is acceptable, however. We must also be willing to challenge (and nonviolently resist if necessary) any tradition or group that is in violation of differentiation, interiority, or communion.

Earth's religions are each beginning to see themselves anew in the light of this evolutionary cosmology. Tribal peoples will naturally find it easiest because, as Brian Swimme notes, "This story, though it comes from the empirical scientific tradition, corroborates in profound and surprising ways the ecological vision of Earth celebrated in every traditional native spirituality of every continent." Some traditions may not find it so easy. Muslims and Jews, for example, are finding it no less unsettling than we are to concede that the natural world is the primary scripture. They, too, are struggling to reinterpret their respective traditions in light of the revelations of reality made possible by the scientific tradition. The new cosmology, because it is both scientifically and mythologically true, will, in time, open up the deeper meanings of every true religious tradition. Or to put it another way, now that the consciousness of Earth is beginning to recognize itself, the planet's spiritual life is able to enter into a whole new level of maturity.

What is the next step for Christians and ecumenism? Perhaps we must first humble ourselves and invite the native and tribal traditions (derogatorily labeled "pagans") to join us in ecumenical dialogue and celebration. That might mean being willing to apologize to them for taking and raping their land and for our attitudes and behavior toward them over the past centuries. Although it may be that we could not have done otherwise, given our cosmology, the witness of scripture and tradition indicates that a little humility goes a long way toward healing, reconciliation, and mutual spiritual growth.

A Native American prophecy circulated widely among the persecuted tribes of the mid-nineteenth century: "The time will come when the sons and daughters of our oppressors will return to us and say, 'Teach us so that we might survive, for we have almost ruined the Earth now.'" More than 100 years later this prophecy is now coming true. There is much that we can learn from our Native American brothers and sisters. If we accomplish this quickly, our children and all the future life forms of this solar system will be eternally grateful.

In our ecumenical endeavors, as in every area of life, we must abide by the three laws of differentiation, subjectivity, and communion. Consider what Thomas Berry has suggested: "The main task of the immediate future is to assist in the intercommunion of all living and nonliving beings in the emerging ecological age of Earth's development. What is most needed to accomplish this task is the great art of intimacy and distance: the capacity of beings (and traditions) to be totally present to each other while further affirming and enhancing the differences and identities of each."

☙ *We must not only learn to tolerate our differences. We must welcome them as the richness and diversity which can lead to true intelligence.* —Albert Einstein

☙ *Have you not learned the most in your life from those with*

whom you disagreed—those who saw it differently than you?
—Walt Whitman

The Apocalypse

❧ Seeing Earth from a distance has changed my perception of the solar system as well. Ever since Copernicus's theory gained wide acceptance, people have considered it an irrefutable truth; yet I submit that we still cling emotionally to the pre-Copernican, or Ptolemaic notion that Earth is the center of everything. —Michael Collins, astronaut

From the perspective of the old cosmology, the apocalypse was often interpreted as the final showdown between good and evil before the destruction of the world and the coming of the heavenly Jerusalem. From the perspective of the new cosmology, however, we know that even if humanity causes its own extinction, the universe will continue. The only difference would be that, of all the planets in the more than 100 billion solar systems of each of the 100 billion galaxies in the universe, this one, at least, would no longer be aware that it was alive.

Understanding the apocalypse as the struggle between good and evil at the end of time is an unnecessary trivialization of the meaning and significance of this Christian truth. The apocalypse is always! It is an ongoing aspect of the will of God in the universe. Cells in a body die every second so that the larger body can live. We are called to do the same. Each moment we must let go of what has brought us to where we are, and have faith (trust) that what is evolving from it is God's will, even if it is uncomfortable.

Faith in God—trust in the universe or faith in nature—is essential for a maturing spirituality. The apocalypse shows that to reach the next stage of maturity, whether individually or as a species, there must be a willingness to let go of the familiar in order to be resurrected to new life and new hope. To have faith is to choose to have hope. It is being willing to trust that, no matter how chaotic the baptism of fire, no matter how tempting Satan's offers in the wilderness, and no matter how painful the crucifixion, God is still in control.

The lack of faith breeds fear, despair, skepticism, cynicism, bitterness, hatred, scheming, selfishness, and manipulation. Gone unchecked, this failure to trust that reality is unfolding according to God's will can lead to evil. Evil can be understood as being aligned with the forces of violence, chaos, and destruction in the universe. It flows in the opposite direction of evolution. Evil works against the Christification of the universe, as Teilhard de Chardin would say.

The battle between good and evil is necessary in a universe with free will. If creation can think reflexively, the decision of whether or not to surrender to God's will is a real one. We need not despair for our children, however. If the apocalyptic literature of the Bible is inspired and true, and if evolution continues as it has, then the chaos and violence integral to the universe is limited, and ultimately transformed, by the larger arc of creative evolution. Thus, we have excellent reason to believe that God will lead us out of the present slavery of industrial consumerism, through the desert of humility and change, and into the promised land.

What is the promised land? Some might identify it as "Thy kingdom come, thy will be done, on Earth as it is in heaven." Others might call it "the ecological age of Earth's development." These are different expressions for similar realities. Though we ourselves may not enter or dwell in the promised land, we can have faith that our children and our grandchildren will.

ᴪ Beloved, do not believe every spirit, but test the spirits to see whether they are from God, for many false prophets have gone out into the world....Beloved, let us love one another, because

love is from God. Everyone who loves is born of God and knows God. Whoever does not love does not know God, for God is love. Those who live in love live in God, and God lives in them.
—1 John 4:1ff

The Kingdom of God

☙ *Once, having been asked by the Pharisees when the kingdom would come, Jesus replied, "The kingdom of God will not come visibly, nor will people say 'Here it is,' or 'There it is,' because the kingdom of God is within [or among] you."*
—Luke 17:20-21

The kingdom of God is an important theological concept in the Bible. Its potency seldom breaks in upon modern hearers, though, since it is usually interpreted in an otherworldly, literal, and patriarchal way. If "the kingdom" is understood as a place, a location in some heavenly world, and if "God" is understood as a transcendent, father-like entity, then the transformational and healing power of this biblical concept will have been almost entirely lost.

It is important to realize that when the biblical writers used the phrase "the kingdom of God," they did not so much mean a location in space as they meant a dimension of reality, an era of living, a reign of truth. Likewise, when Moses, the prophets, Jesus, or the apostles used the phrase "God," they probably did not mean a "super being" who lived far off in a "super place" and who caused "ordinary beings" down here to exist or change. "When the Bible or classical theology referred to 'God' as an individual person," says theologian Gene Marshall, "this was a pictorial way of talking about 'reality in all its fullness.'" God is not the greatest or largest of beings; God is the ground of *all* being. God is that awesome and mysterious Reality in which all things live and move and have their being, and out of which all things emerge and into which all things return.

A number of theologians are now suggesting that the best way to translate "the kingdom of God" so that modern hearers can experience its prophetic power and authority is "the reign of Reality." If we grant that this may be a faithful translation, we can see that to live in the reign of Reality means living in faith, trusting that Reality is like a loving, forgiving parent. It means abiding in the realm of truth, honesty, integrity, love, and compassion. To live outside the reign of Reality (in hell, essentially) is to live in fear, illusion, falsity, selfishness, pride, or dishonesty. The reign of Reality is not a place ruled by an otherworldly Being. It is a dimension of earthly life where truth, justice, and love are valued above all else, and where evolution is advancing with choice and free will. This interpretation helps us grasp some of the deeper meaning behind Jesus' prophetic call, "Repent, for the kingdom of God is at hand!"

☙ *Jesus said, "Except you be converted, and become as little children, you shall not enter into the kingdom of heaven."*
—Matthew 18:3

☙ *The disciples asked, "When will the kingdom come?" Jesus replied, "The kingdom will not come by expectation. Nor will it do to say, 'Here it is!' or 'There it is!' Rather the kingdom of heaven is spread out on Earth, but people do not see it."*
—Gospel of Thomas, 112

Heaven and Hell

☙ *Not less but more than Dante, we know for certain that there is a heaven and a hell—a heaven, when a good deed has been done, a hell, in the dark heart able to no longer live openly.*
—Edward Dowden

☙ *O Lord, where can I go from your spirit? Or where can I flee from your presence? If I ascend to heaven, you are there; if I make my bed in hell, you are there.* —David (Psalm 139:7–8)

However varied their interpretation throughout the Bible and church history, heaven and hell have been central concepts within the Christian tradition. And well they should be, for they point to eternal truths. In the old cosmology, however, they were often thought of as actual places in an otherworldly realm. The poetic language used to describe them was often taken literally: heaven with its mansions and pearly gates, no crying and no dying; hell with its fiery pit, weeping and gnashing of teeth.

Modern society has found such literalism increasingly unbelievable and meaningless. In response to this, Christians have sometimes argued that such truths simply needed to be accepted "on faith." But "faith" in the Bible is usually synonymous with "trust": a willingness to let go of the familiar and know that God (i.e., Reality) will prove trustworthy and faithful. Lack of faith is shown by individuals or groups who try to manipulate reality toward what they perceive as good, right, or orthodox. To have faith means trusting that all things work together for the good of those who live realistically, who love the truth. The idea of "faith" as believing in what does not make any sense is more a reaction against the scientific worldview than it is a biblical notion.

As it is written, "The just (or righteous) shall live by faith." —Paul (Romans 1:17)

Jesus said, "Your faith has saved you; go in peace." —Luke 7:50

There is no great future for any people whose faith has burned out. —Rufus M. Jones

ॐ *Our faith imposes on us a right and duty to throw ourselves into the things of the Earth.* — Pierre Teilhard de Chardin

We are now able to appreciate the reality of heaven and hell in ways that do not involve the need to believe in them as literal, otherworldly places. Heaven and hell are living truths that have to do with harmony or disharmony with God's revealed will for the universe. They are eternal realities, which means that they are ongoing and have everything to do with this real world in which we live and move and have our being. They will continue as long as the universe continues to evolve with self-conscious awareness. Heaven and hell are not places; they are dimensions of earthly reality that exist beyond the life of any part of the body.

The traditional view that our experience of heaven or hell is determined by our earthly existence seems accurate. It makes sense that the experience of reality in life affects the experience of reality in death. But the issue is one of consciousness, not location.

Heaven is the experience of being connected and reconciled to the divine. It is the fruit of freely choosing to do what the rest of nature does instinctually. Heaven is being centered in God's will, being a channel of divine grace and creative evolutionary power in the world. Hell, on the other hand, is the experience of being separated from God. It is the fruit of being out of sync with nature and out of step with God's will. Hell is being caught up in fear, cynicism, distrust, selfishness, bitterness, illusion, falsity, hatred, or anything else that keeps us alienated from our larger Self or any part of the body. To be in hell is to be a cell in the body without knowing it, like a cancer cell, and thus cut off from the way, the truth, and the life. To be in heaven is to be aware of one's identity as a cell in the divine body, to surrender to the will of the larger Self of the universe, God, and to be participating in the way, the truth, and the life.

🔸 *Heaven means to be one with God.* —Confucius

🔸 *Paradise is to wish only to be where you are.*
—Bill Joyner

🔸 *Upon this rock I will build my church, and the gates of hell will not prevail against it. I will give you the keys of the kingdom of heaven, and whatever you bind on earth will be bound in heaven, and whatever you loose on earth will be loosed in heaven.* —Jesus (Matthew 16:18–19)

Jesus Christ as the Way, the Truth, and the Life

🔸 *I tell you the truth: those who believe in me will do what I have been doing, and, in fact, will do even greater things than these.* —Jesus (John 14:12)

🔸 *Christ was made human that we might be made God.*
—Athanasius

🔸 *I have been crucified with Christ; it is no longer I who live, but Christ who lives in me.* —Paul (Galatians 2:20)

We can now understand and celebrate the fact that a communion of differentiated subjects has been, is now, and always will be God's will for creation. The natural world, our primary scripture, tells us clearly that this is the case. There are multiple truths in an interdependent relationship at every level of reality. It makes sense to talk about "the Truth" only at the level of the entire body of the universe. If we acknowledge that divine truth is found in other religious traditions and cultures, though, how do we understand Jesus' words, "I am the way, and the truth, and the life; no one comes to the Father except through me" (John 14:6)? That is, in the context of the new cosmology, how is Jesus the embodiment of the way to God, the truth of God, and the life of God?

We must start by recalling that Jesus, like us, was not separate from Earth. Jesus was a conscious expression of this living planet, perhaps the heart of it. As Jesus realized his divinity, as he experienced his Oneness with God, Earth came to that awareness about itself through him. When he learned that unconditional, self-expansive love was the only way to experience the reign of Reality, the whole universe participated in that discovery and was changed forever. When Jesus broke through to the knowledge that he was the only way to God, creation learned that about itself in him. "In Christ all things hold together" (Colossians 1:17). Through the differentiated personality of Jesus, the universe experienced in consciousness the fact that it was an incarnation of God! This awareness became forever available to us because of him. Biblical metaphors such as Christ being "the firstborn of creation" or "the head of the body" point to this. Everything changed forever through the life, death, and resurrection of Jesus Christ. As the early Christians expressed it, Jesus was, is, and always will be Lord.

When Jesus said that he was the way, the truth, and the life, and that no one could come to God except through him, he was speaking a profound and eternal truth that is tragically misunderstood if we think that only Christians are going to heaven (as if heaven were a place to go to).

Jesus embodied the Way. That is, whether a person is a Buddhist, Hindu, Muslim, Taoist, Confucian, or Native American, the only way to live in the reign of Reality is to live, like Jesus, a life of humility, integrity, and self-expansive love of the wider community of life. Any other "way" is a deception.

Jesus embodied Truth. He showed that truth is an integral part of the way to God. Thus, pride, deception, fear, and selfishness have no place in the reign of Reality. Jesus modeled the fact that truthfulness is an essential quality of realistic living.

God reigns wherever truth reigns. Like Jesus, we too can be one with the truth if we align ourselves with the will of our larger Self, the living Earth.

Jesus embodied Life. He was fully and eternally alive, and showed us by word and example how we too might experience life eternally. Jesus lived within the laws that enabled the universe to develop, embodying the life and will of God. He participated in the triune life of God through his obedience to the divine will. Thanks to him, we are now capable of the same. But we have a choice: if we follow in his footsteps we are promised eternal life, and the evolution of this planet will continue with reflective awareness. If we merely worship him as an idol, without following the way, the truth, and the life he modeled, we will perish in the wilderness.

❦ *Whoever drinks from my mouth will become like me and I shall be that person, and what is hidden shall be revealed.*
—Jesus (The Gospel of Thomas, 106)

❦ *Though we are God's sons and daughters, we do not realize it yet.* —Meister Eckhart

❦ *With very few exceptions, Christian churches have never entertained the prospect of humans actually being or becoming like Jesus in all respects. Yet the New Testament is replete with evidence of his call to others to follow him and become like him in all respects. Were this not so, then his injunctions and teachings ("You must be perfect, as your heavenly Father is perfect" [Matthew 5:48]) would constitute a self-conscious mockery of human potential.* —Douglas Bowman

Questions for Reflection and Discussion

1. What were your favorite quotes in this chapter? Why?

2. What did you find most exciting in this chapter? Most challenging? Most insightful? Most disturbing? Why?

3. Was there anything in Chapter 3 about which you might say, "At some level I think that I have always known this; I've just never thought about it like that or put it in those words"? If so, what was it?

4. If teenagers and young people were taught Christianity according to the new cosmology, what effect do you think it might have on their involvement in the church? Why?

5. What are some of the ways in which "the second coming of Christ" might be understood from the perspective of the new cosmology? How have you understood it in the past? What does it mean to you now?

6. What are some other examples of "different expressions for similar realities"? Why do you suppose this is so common in everyday life?

7. What are some other doctrinal or theological areas that might look differently in light of the new cosmology? How so?

8. What do you understand as the major differences between following Jesus "in his steps" and making an idol out of him? Do you agree that this is a life and death matter? Why or why not?

❧ 4 ❧

What Does It Mean to Be Christian Today?

❧ *A tree is recognized by its fruit.* —Jesus (Matthew 12:33)

Essential Christianity

❧ *If you hold to my teaching, you are really my disciples. Then you will know the truth, and* the truth will set you free.
—Jesus (John 8:32)

Much theological fog is now evaporating like an early morning mist in the light of the dawning new cosmology. The path of Jesus Christ is not and never has been one of exclusivism or escapism; it is profoundly oriented toward life. The religion known as Christianity, however, is faithful to the Spirit of Christ, the Holy Spirit, only to the extent that it is willing to let go of its institutional forms and obey the radical call of Jesus: "Come, follow me." The following is an outline of an understanding of Christianity that is faithful to the Bible, tradition, and the new cosmology.

Christianity can be understood as a call to forsake sin, illusion, and selfishness, and to surrender to the reality of faith, hope, and love. It calls us to see the divine in every-thing that lives and supports life, and empowers us to love what we see with all our heart, mind, soul, and strength. It challenges us to make a wholehearted com-mitment to truth, justice, and peace, and to live in a mutu-ally enhancing relationship with the entire natural world. It is an invitation to be honest and vulnerable, trusting Re-ality to be like a forgiving, loving parent. It is a call for us to realize that our larger Self is the entire community of life—past, present, and future, including our enemies—and that to live in the reign of God we must love it all as God in Christ loved us. In short, Christianity is a sum-mons to be Christ-centered and Christ-like in every area of life, respecting every form of life.

Jesus Christ gave himself in sacrificial love for the salvation of the cosmos. He showed us that the way to experience life eternally was to live with an expansive sense of Self and in ac-cordance with God's will. The destiny of Christianity is inextri-cably linked to following Jesus and enfleshing the reign of Re-ality as we participate in the emerging ecological age. But as we have said, Jesus didn't do it all for us; he showed us the only way to do it. We are each called to take up our cross and walk in his steps as a bodily incarnation of God's grace among a people who do not yet know their true nature and destiny.

The human family must, implicitly at least, follow Jesus or perish. It is that simple. Reality is saying that the salvation or damnation of all future generations is in our hands. If Chris-tians worldwide will live ecologically Christ-centered and Christ-like, our children will be saved; Earth will continue to flourish with life and awareness. If we wait for Jesus to return and rescue us, or if we think that ecological concerns are not the church's primary business, our children will be lost. Earth will go on without humanity.

We are standing at a pivotal moment in our 15-billion-year history. We are called to evangelize the world through living and proclaiming the good news of the new cosmology. May we be as faithful to the revelation given us as the early Christians were to the revelation given them.

❦ *Let the same mind be in you that you have in Christ Jesus: Who, though he was in the form of God, did not regard equality with God as something to be grasped, but emptied himself, taking the very nature of a servant, being born in human likeness. And being found in human form, he humbled himself and became obedient unto death—even death on a cross. Therefore God has also highly exalted him and bestowed on him the name which is above every name, that at the name of Jesus every knee should bend in heaven and earth and under the earth, and every tongue confess that Jesus Christ is Lord to the glory of God the Father.* —Paul (Philippians 2:9–11)

❦ *Humanity has reached the biological point where it must either lose all belief in the universe or quite resolutely worship it. This is where we must look for the origin of the present crisis in morality....Henceforth the world will only kneel before the organic center of its evolution.* —Pierre Teilhard de Chardin

❦ *A morality of reverence will also be a morality of responsibility—not a responsibility based on duty and fear of disobedience but a responsibility based on care for what we cherish and revere.* —Matthew Fox

❦ *What the world desperately needs is information and heightened consciousness, the awareness of the fact that the global environmental crisis is the primary and most crucial issue the world currently faces. That crisis should constitute the primary agenda item for all our institutions—from the churches to gov-*

ernment. *Indeed, it may be argued that the current pathology of all our institutions—including the churches—is evidenced in their refusal, for a variety of reasons, to make the environmental issue their principal agenda item....I would argue that the greatest service the churches could render the world at this time is providing education concerning facts of the environmental crisis, the ingredients in our thinking and action that have contributed to the crisis, and the resources we already have available to us for altering our way of thinking and action in constructive ways.* —Douglas Bowman

Acknowledging Our Struggle

When our days become dreary with low-hovering clouds and our nights become darker than a thousand midnights, we will know that we are living in the creative turmoil of a genuine civilization struggling to be born. —Martin Luther King, Jr.

Where do we go from here? For most of us, the first thing to do is to acknowledge our discomfort and confess our personal resistance to making changes of the magnitude that humanity is now called upon to make. Normally, such shifts might take a few hundred years at least. But Earth is telling us that we do not have that much time. Future generations cry out to us. The air, water, and soil cry out to us. The dying species cry out to us. As Jesus said, "Let anyone who has ears to hear listen!"

Like the Israelites of old, we must trust God to guide us through the wilderness into the promised land. Such large shifts in thinking about God, ourselves, and our world are not easy to make. Yet make them we must if we are to avoid planetary suicide. Every person, religion, system of government, and human institution is now being confronted with the truth of who we are and where God wills us to go. The next few decades will see worldwide changes that we can scarcely imagine now. This will be deeply unsettling for the human family as a whole. That is why we need each other's love and prayerful support, as well as a steadfast faith that God is guiding the process. The Israelites wandered for forty years in the desert before God allowed them to enter the promised land. This must have been most difficult for them. But God was faithful...and still is.

We are at a critical turning point in history. A worldwide, Earth-oriented, religious revival seems to be a growing possibility in the relatively near future. Let us earnestly and unceasingly pray for this...for our children's sake.

As the turning point approaches, the realization that evolutionary changes of this magnitude cannot be prevented by short-term political activities provides our strongest hope for the future. —Fritjof Capra

Here we might observe that the basic mood of the future might well be one of confidence in the continuing revelation that takes place in and through the earth. If the dynamics of the universe from the beginning shaped the course of the heavens, lighted the sun, and formed the earth, if this same dynamism brought forth the continents and seas and atmosphere, if it awakened life in the primordial cell and then brought into being the unnumbered variety of living beings, and finally brought us into being and guided us safely through the turbulent centuries, there is reason to believe that this same guiding process is precisely what has awakened in us our present understanding of ourselves and our relation to this stupendous process. Sensitized to such guidance from the very structure and functioning of the universe, we can have confidence in the future that awaits the human venture. —Thomas Berry

What a time to be alive! Humankind has dawning upon its

consciousness a new perception of its origins—the nature of life, the world, the universe, God....We stand on the threshold of a new time for the earth, for we are confronted with the prospect of taking a new evolutionary step. We are challenged to enter into a new life by the prospect of adopting a new way of thinking. —Douglas Bowman

Faith, Hope, and Love

🙢 *Beloved, we are now children of God; what we will be has not yet been revealed. What we do know is this: when it is revealed we will be like him, for we will see him as he is. And all who have this hope purify themselves, just as he is pure.*
—1 John 3:2–3

🙢 *This is our hope: that the children born today may still have, twenty years hence, a bit of green grass under their bare feet, a breath of clean air to breathe, a patch of blue water to sail upon, and a whale on the horizon to set them dreaming.*
—Jacques Cousteau

🙢 *In our every deliberation, we must consider the impact of our decisions on the next seven generations.* —From the Great Law of the Six Nations Iroquois Confederacy

As we pick up our cross to follow Jesus, let us learn from those who plant dates. A date tree takes eighty years from the time it is planted to bear its first fruit. To plant a date tree is an act of faith, a sign of hope, and a symbol of one's loving commitment to the future. There is a message here for us all. For if there is anything that Christianity at its best stands for it is realistic faith, hope, and love. Brazilian theologian Rubem Alves saw this clearly when he said: "What is hope? It is the presentiment that imagination is more real and reality less real than it looks. It is the hunch that the overwhelming brutality of facts that oppress and repress are not the last word. It is the suspicion that reality is more complex than realism wants us to believe; that the frontiers of the possible are not determined by the limits of the actual, and that in a miraculous and unexpected way, life is preparing the creative events which will open the way to freedom and resurrection.

"The two, suffering and hope, live from each other. Suffering without hope produces resentment and despair. Hope without suffering creates illusions, naiveté, and drunkenness.

"Let us plant dates, even though we who plant them will never eat them...We must live by the love of what we will never see. This is the secret discipline. It is the refusal to let our creative act be dissolved away in immediate sense experience, and is a stubborn commitment to the future of our grandchildren. Such disciplined love is what has given prophets, revolutionaries, and saints the courage to die for the future they envisaged. They make their own bodies the seed of their highest hopes."

✌ *So let's plant dates!* —Miriam MacGillis

✌ *Most of the people I talk with feel we have a fighting chance to stop environmental destruction within 50 years and to turn the culture around within 800 to 1000 years. "Fighting chance" translates as long odds but good company, and bioregionalism is obviously directed at people with a little gamble in their blood. Since we won't live to see the results of this hoped for transformation, we might as well start it right, with the finest expressions of spirit and style we can muster, keeping in mind that there is only a functional difference between the flower and the root, that essentially they are part of the same abiding faith....The sun still rises every morning. Dig in.*
—Jim Dodge

❧ *The dream drives the action.* —Thomas Berry

❧ *The future belongs to those who give the next generation reasons to hope.* —Pierre Teilhard de Chardin

Questions for Reflection and Discussion

1. What were your favorite quotes in this chapter? Why?

2. What did you find most exciting in this chapter? Most challenging? Most insightful? Most disturbing? Why?

3. Was there anything in Chapter 4 about which you might say, "At some level I think that I have always known this; I've just never thought about it like that or put it in those words"? If so, what was it?

4. Do you think that our children and grandchildren are likely to experience this message as gospel, that is, as a realistic hope of salvation from the actual bad news they face? Why or why not?

5. Do you agree or disagree with the author's understanding of the core of Christianity in this chapter? What changes might you make?

6. What would it mean in practical, down-to-earth terms for you to plant dates?

7. Jim Dodge suggests that "we have a fighting chance to stop environmental destruction within 50 years and to turn the culture around within 800 to 1000 years." Do you agree or disagree? Why?

❧ 5 ❧

Transformed by Renewing Our Mind

❧ *Do not be conformed to this age any longer, but be transformed by the renewing of your mind, so that you may be able to discern what is the will of God—what is good and acceptable and perfect.* —Paul (Romans 12:2)

Developing the Habit of Being the Planet

❧ *The day will come when, after mastering the wind, the waves, the tides and gravity, we shall harness for God the energies of love. And on that day, for the second time in the history of the world, humanity will have discovered fire.*
—Pierre Teilhard de Chardin

❧ *Through the wider Self every living being is connected intimately, and from this intimacy follows the capacity of identification and its natural consequences, the practice of nonviolence.*
—Arne Naess

❧ *Our understanding must grow to encompass a union of nature and culture in which the sacredness of all life is honored.*

*As long as we saw all other life as outside and apart from our-
selves, we treated it carelessly. Embracing the interconnectedness of all life, we can again weave together the rift between
sacred and secular, and the totality will be seen as sacred.*
—Nancy Jack Todd and John Todd

Until this cosmology becomes habitual, and until we see all
of life this way without thinking about it, we cannot fully experience its transforming power or enjoy its fruit. This is true of
individuals, of the church, and of the species as a whole. This
shift in consciousness, from thinking about the planet to thinking *as* the planet, must become deeply ingrained in order to experience it as gospel. It must dwell in our hearts, not merely
our minds. It is only as we feel a deep sense of personal connection to the evolutionary process, and develop the habit of
thinking and feeling from the perspective of the larger body of
life that we will become incarnations of God's saving grace.

(William Prescott, a planetary therapist, has developed a
number of exercises that are designed to promote this kind of
habitual awareness. I will share a few of them here, and recommend his article "Being the Planet" in the Winter 1985/86 issue
of *In Context*.)

One practice that many have found helpful in developing
the habit of thinking as the planet is to reflect occasionally during the day: "How are my actions or inactions affecting the
ecology of my larger Self? How are my thoughts affecting the
mental ecology of the planet? How are my emotions affecting
the emotional ecology of the planet?" To insure that this is a
fruitful exercise, though, it is important to be gentle, loving, patient, and forgiving with yourself as you do it.

As a meditation exercise, practice expanding your awareness and self-identification until you encompass the globe. Sit
comfortably with your eyes closed. Imaginatively open your
heart and soul more and more until it becomes one with Earth

and you feel compassionate love for every part of your Self. Then, while maintaining the perspective of the planet as a whole, open your eyes and look around. Notice what you've never noticed before. Listen carefully. Feel the awe and mystery that accompanies this level of awareness. Think about whatever personal, local, or global issues may be important to you as you continue to feel the expansive love of God within and around you. Then write down your insights and feelings. When we practice "becoming the planet" in this way, we realize what is in fact already the case. We experience ourselves as the self-conscious heart, mind, and eyes of the living Earth.

ᶺ *A human being is part of the whole, called by us "universe," a part limited in time and space. We experience ourselves, our thoughts and feelings, as something separated from the rest—a kind of optical delusion of our consciousness. This delusion is a kind of prison for us, restricting us to our personal desires and to affection for a few persons nearest to us. Our task must be to free ourselves from this prison by widening our circle of compassion to embrace all living creatures and the whole of nature in its beauty.* —Albert Einstein

ᶺ *We are here to embrace rather than conquer the world.* —Patsey Hallen

ᶺ *We are as large as our loves.* —Baruch Spinoza

Another widely used practice is to keep an "Earth diary" in which you note the major ways you have affected the planet on a given day, considering these changes from your point of view. Then go through the exercise of "becoming the planet," embrace Earth, and look at the ways you affected the planet from the planet's point of view. Make changes based on what the larger body of life wants or needs.

ᴥ The ecological self of a person is that with which a person identifies. —Arne Naess

ᴥ Ecological consciousness is the result of a psychological expansion of the narrowly encapsulated sense of self as isolated ego, through identification with all humans (species chauvinism), to finally an awareness of identification and interpenetration of self with ecosystem and biosphere. —George Sessions

Meditations/Affirmations for Life

ᴥ Passion and enthusiasm are no substitutes for discipline, integrity, and faithfulness. — Brian Patrick

ᴥ The Logos of God has become human so that you might learn from a human being how a human being may become divine. —Clement of Alexandria

In developing any habit it can be helpful to have daily reminders. The following meditations, or affirmations, may assist you in integrating the new creation story. As you read or think about any one of these statements, take a moment in prayerful silence to see if God wants to emphasize something or deepen your awareness in some way. Consider the statement long enough to feel it within you. Notice how your experience of reality is affected. Internalized, these meditations can become a part of the natural way that you see and experience the world. They can serve to strengthen your faith, deepen your relationship with your true Self, and help you become more ecologically Christ-centered and Christ-like. (Modify them in any way that you find helpful.) The "Prayer for Life" on pages 84–85 is based on these meditations/affirmations.

1. I am the sum total of 15 billion years of unbroken evolutionary development now thinking about itself. I am becoming aware of the awesome implications of my Story.

2. I am an interdependent cell within the body of Earth. The entire living universe is my larger Self. Everything I see, hear, and feel is a part of me.

3. I feel the loving support of God's presence. I am aware that my breathing, seeing, hearing, and feeling are acts of communion and prayer. Everything I see, hear, and feel reveals God, is a face of the divine.

4. I am deepening my awareness of Reality and growing spiritually as I develop the habit of saying to myself, no matter what the context or circumstances, "This is a divine revelation. This is my larger Self."

5. I am participating in the further evolution of the universe through love. I know that everything I say and do, or fail to say or do, affects future generations.

6. I am committed to the Way, the Truth, and the Life. I peacefully yet firmly oppose those who disregard or violate the divine laws of differentiation (diversity), interiority (personality), or communion (interrelationship).

7. Everything that happens is perfect in the sense that it provides the maximum opportunity for my growth and learning. There is only feedback and learning; no failure.

8. I can accept myself and others completely here and now. I am aware that we each tend to do the best we can, given the internal and external resources available to us at the time.

9. I have everything I need to fully enjoy the present. I can take full responsibility, with thanksgiving, for everything I am experiencing.

10. I feel with compassion the problems and opportunities of others without getting snagged in those things that are offering them messages for their own growth. I don't need to fix, heal, or convert anyone. If needed, I can trust that God will...in nature's perfect timing.

11. Every moment is a one-time grace gift of God. I may not live to see the sun rise or set again. I act only when centered,

loving, and aware of my interconnectedness, and postpone acting when otherwise.

12. Every moment, no matter what the situation or circumstances, I have a choice between two paths: the path of resentment, denial, judgment, doubt, fear, and control, or the path of gratitude, acceptance, trust, faith, hope, and love. One path is hellish, the other heavenly.

13. I listen humbly and carefully to others who are different from me. I affirm and enhance the differences of others while I remain faithful to the truth as I understand and experience it.

14. I am empowered by the realization that we are always creating memories. I am developing the habit of asking myself, "What would I have to do, or not do, in order to feel great about this day tomorrow? a week for now? a year from now?"

15. I am becoming more Christ-like and Christ-centered as I regularly ask myself, "What would Jesus think about this?" and, "What would Jesus say or do in this situation?" and then say or do it.

16. I am in direct contact with the source and energy of my Being, and gain both strength and humility, as I remind myself throughout the day that "I am a cell in the universe."

⁓ *Certainly one of the most accurate ways to understand the divine in our day is to see God as the Self of the universe.*
—Brian Patrick

⁓ *We are meant to become more like God.* —Aquinas

⁓ *God became a human being in order that human beings might become God.* —Iranaeus

Updating Our Mental Scrapbook

⁓ *A mistake in one's understanding of Creation will necessarily cause a mistake in one's understanding of God.* —Aquinas

꙳ Most of our notions about the world come from a set of assumptions which we take for granted, and which, for the most part, we don't examine or question. We bring these assumptions to the table with us as a given. They are so much a part of who we are that it is difficult for us to separate ourselves from them enough to be able to talk about them. We do not think about these assumptions, we think from them.
—Werner Erhard

Philosopher and historian Thomas Kuhn once remarked, "When paradigms change, the world changes with them." These are unsettling times because we are in the midst of a great paradigm shift. Recent discoveries in the natural sciences have led to a new understanding of reality. The most fundamental ways that we have of understanding ourselves, our world, and how God relates to the whole process are shifting. We must now update our internal imagery to fit what we empirically know to be true. The reason this is essential is because our unconscious pictures of reality influence us far more than the abstract concepts we say we believe.

For example, although Christianity has long affirmed both the transcendence of God (God is more than creation, the Creator and source of everything) and the immanence of God (God is the pulsing reality and living energy within everything), most Christians have been able to imagine only transcendence. And what cannot be pictured in the mind's eye generally remains an impotent abstraction. It is one thing to agree with Paul when he says, "There is one God...who is over all and through all and in all" (Ephesians 4:6) or "In God we live and move and have our being" (Acts 17:28). It is another thing to be able to imagine how this is so. But unless these truths can be imaged, they cannot change or empower us.

The mental pictures that most of us have unconsciously held of ourselves in relation to God and the rest of creation were

Prayer for Life

Dear God, please allow me to be ever aware that you are the divine wholeness of Reality in which I live and move and have my being. Remind me often of our larger evolutionary story, and allow me to continually grow in my understanding of its implications. Help me to experience everything as a revelation of you and as part of my larger Self. Oh God, may I be a channel of your loving energy to other parts of the body. Please help me to remember that everything I say or do, or fail to say or do, affects future generations. Empower me to respectfully question and, if need be, peacefully oppose those who disregard or violate differentiation, interiority, and communion.

God, help me to know and feel that everything that happens is perfect in the sense that it provides the maximum opportunity for my growth and learning. Help me to accept myself and others completely here and now, remembering that we each tend to do the best we can given the internal and external resources we have available to us at the time. Help me to forgive, to let go, and to trust that your will is unfolding naturally.

God, help me to remember that I have everything I need to fully enjoy the present, and help me to take personal responsibility, with thanksgiving, for everything I experience. May I feel with compassion and the problems and opportunities of others, without trying to fix, heal, or convert them. Help me to have faith in you and to patiently trust in nature's timing.

God, please allow me to live with the awareness that every moment is a one-time gift of grace, and that I may not live to see the sun rise or set again. Help me to act only when centered, loving, and aware of my interconnectedness, and to postpone acting when otherwise. Help me to affirm and enhance the differences of others while remaining faithful to the truth as I understand and experience it. May I be a careful and sensitive listener. May I live in ever increasing harmony with all of Nature.

God, please help me to know that every moment, no matter what the situation or circumstances, I have a choice between heaven and hell; between the path of gratitude, acceptance, trust, faith, hope, love and the path of resentment, denial, judgment, doubt, fear, and control. Please develop in me the habit of asking myself, "What kind of yesterday am I creating by my actions or inaction today?" and, "What would I have to do or not do in order to feel great about this day tomorrow? a week from now? a year from now?" Likewise, help me to naturally and regularly ask, "What would Jesus think about, do or say in this situation?" and then give me the expansive love and courage to do or say it, remembering that I am a cell in the universe.

Dear God, daily give me the wisdom and strength to fight my greatest enemy—my*self*. And help me to remember that my greatest ally in this battle is my*Self*.

Amen.

based on the old cosmology. As paradigms, these images have influenced every facet of life in the West. But we must now update our internal imagery, integrating the new cosmology. If we are to be faithful to the truth as we now understand it, our mental images must reflect the awareness that we are the latest development of a process that has been spiritual from the beginning, and that we are part of an organic, living universe in which everything is interrelated and interdependent. The following sketches illustrate the difference between the old and new cosmologies.

The Old Cosmology

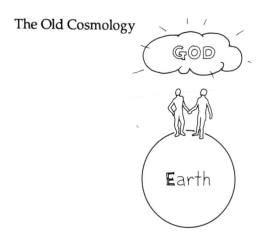

Westerners have generally imagined God as transcendent to creation, as illustrated above. We saw ourselves as separate from and above the rest of nature also, for we intuitively knew that we were created in God's image. We believed that we lived *on* a planet that we were to be stewards of. What was important was our relationship to God and our relationship to other human beings. Though Earth was the stage upon which this drama was played out, it was not an integral part of things.

Western economics, law, and ethics each function out of this view of reality. Morality, for example, has been concerned with human behavior only toward God and each other, but treatment of Earth has not generally been considered a moral issue. Corporations can legally poison the air, water, and soil, and forests and species can be obliterated because our morality and laws are human-centered rather than life-centered.

The New Cosmology

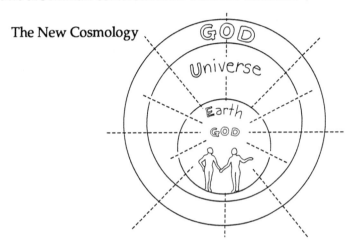

The new cosmology sees God as intimately revealed in the diversity of creation, yet infinitely more than the whole of creation. Humans are recognized as an integral part of Earth, not superior to it. The new cosmology and the old cosmology agree that the most important thing for humans is our relationship to God. But there are two important differences in how this is understood. In the new cosmology, God is acknowledged to be embodied in creation rather than separate from it. And in the new cosmology the "our" in "our relationship to God" is the entire community of life, rather than humans in isolation. We are deceived if we think that we can love God and honor God's holiness without loving others (human and non-human) and honoring the holiness of nature (see 1 John 4:20–21).

The universe reveals God. Nature is a showing forth of divinity. Therefore, praising and glorifying God has everything to do with humanity being that part of creation which enables the body to appreciate its beauty and celebrate its divinity. The old cosmology said, "Worship the Creator, not creation." It must have been important for Western humanity to believe that dichotomy. But times are different now. The new cosmology says, "If we don't worship the Creator in and through creation, our "worship" will lead to death rather than life.

Another difference between these cosmologies is the way each understands the organization of creation. The following diagram is an example of what is sometimes referred to as the Western hierarchy of value.

The Old Cosmology

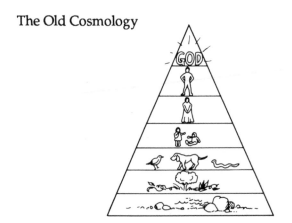

Most of us learned to see the value of things in an unchanging, patriarchal, and hierarchical way. God was Father; men were superior to women; male children were more important than female children; animals were above plants; plants were above insects, worms, and bacteria; and at the bottom of the pyramid were the inanimate rocks and elements of Earth. We believed that this was the way God set things up in the beginning and intended that they remain. Although we have been rarely conscious of it, most Western institutions assume this perspective. But we now see things quite differently.

The New Cosmology

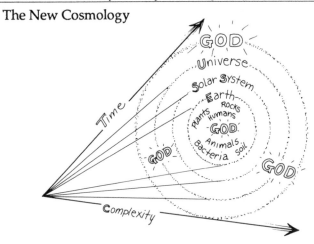

The new cosmology understands that everything is changing, that we are part of a time-developmental universe. As time
continues, creation becomes more complex and more capable
of realizing its inner, spiritual potential. In other words, the
universe is maturing. God is seen as both transcendent and im-
manent. Everything that makes up Earth is seen equally as a
revelation of God and necessary for the healthy functioning of
the body. We are each part of a living communion of diverse
personalities bound together in an inseparable relationship in
space and time. Humans have no existence outside of the ecological cycles of Earth, which in turn has no existence outside
of the solar system. The solar system has no existence outside
the Milky Way galaxy. The Milky Way has no existence outside of the universe. And the universe has no existence outside
of God. Everything is totally interrelated and interdependent.
God's immanence makes the entire process divine.

Finally, it makes a world of difference—literally— how we
perceive an individual human being in our imagination. From
the old perspective, a farmer might be imagined something
like this:

The Old Cosmology

This illustration is a misleading abstraction. There is no such thing as an isolated human being—except in our imagination. Any human in actual existence exists *only* as a member of the wider community of life, air, water, and soil. To think of ourselves as separate from the rest of nature as we have may have been important for our evolutionary development. To continue seeing ourselves this way any longer, however, is suicidal. The following image is a truer depiction of a farmer.

The New Cosmology

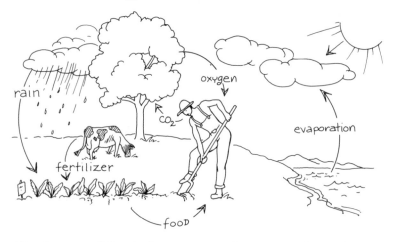

Our true condition is that we are each an integral member of the entire life community. We are neither stewards, nor care-takers, nor anything else that assumes we are separate from na-ture. We have no existence apart from the living Earth. We are Earth. We are the self-conscious and spiritually aware organi-zation of elements of this living planet. We are totally depen-dent upon the health of the wider community of life for our own health. Our own destiny, as individuals or as a species, and the destiny of Earth are identical. What we do to Earth, we do to our Self.

As our mental images of reality reflect the new cosmology, we will find it much easier to integrate it into our daily lives. We will also experience God's loving presence and transform-ing power in a way that was impossible as long as we were op-erating from unconscious images of the old cosmology.

↊ *Indeed, I consider that this shift [to an emphasis on our ca-pacity to identify with the larger collective of all beings] is es-sential to our survival at this point in history precisely because it can serve in lieu of morality and because moralizing is inef-fective. Sermons seldom hinder us from pursuing our self-interest, so we need to be a little more enlightened about what our self-interest is. It would not occur to me, for example, to ex-hort you to refrain from cutting off your leg. That wouldn't oc-cur to me or to you, because your leg is part of you. Well, so are the trees in the Amazon Basin; they are our external lungs. We are just beginning to wake up to that. We are gradually discov-ering that we are our world.* —Joanna Macy

↊ *Nature is the unseen intelligence that loved us into being.* —Elbert Hubbard

↊ *Divinity is the enfolding and unfolding of everything that is. Divinity is in all things in such a way that all things are in di-vinity.* —Nicholas of Cusa

❧ *Christ exists in all things that are.* —Gregory of Nazianzus

❧ *The Great Spirit is the life that is in all things—all creatures and plants and even rocks and the minerals. All things—and I mean all things—have their own will and their own way and their own purpose.* —Rolling Thunder

❧ *To injure the creature is to injure the Creator, and to love the creature is to love the Creator.* —Douglas Bowman

Earth Looks in the Mirror

❧ **Once a photograph of the Earth, taken from the outside, is available...a new idea as powerful as any in history will be let loose....** —Sir Fred Hoyle, 1948

❧ *Before I flew I was already aware of how small and vulnerable our planet is; but only when I saw it from space, in all its ineffable beauty and fragility, did I realize that humankind's most urgent task is to cherish and preserve it for future generations.* —Sigmund Jahn, astronaut

❧ *Earth reminded us of a Christmas tree ornament hanging in the blackness of space. As we got farther and farther away it diminished in size. Finally, it shrank to the size of a marble, the most beautiful marble you can imagine. That beautiful, warm, living object looked so fragile, so delicate....Seeing this has to change a person, has to make a person appreciate the creation of God and the love of God.* —James Irwin, astronaut

❧ *The Earth is the Lord's and all the fullness thereof, the world, and all those who live in it.* —David (Psalm 24:1)

❧ *During a space flight, the psyche of each astronaut is re-*

shaped. *Having seen the sun, the stars, and our planet, you become more full of life, softer. You begin to look at all living things with greater trepidation and you begin to be more kind and patient with the people around you. At any rate that is what happened to me.* —Boris Volynov, astronaut

⋙ *The first day we all pointed to our own countries. The third or fourth day we were pointing to our continents. By the fifth day we were aware of only one Earth.*
—Prince Sultan bin Salman al-Saud, astronaut

⋙ *It isn't important in which sea or lake you observe a slick of pollution, or in the forests of which country a fire breaks out, or on which continent a hurricane arises. You are standing guard over the whole of our Earth.* —Yuri Artyukhin, astronaut

⋙ *From space, I get the definite, but indescribable feeling that this, my maternal Planet, is somehow actually breathing— faintly sighing in her sleep—ever so slowly winking and wimpling in the benign light of the sun, while her musclelike clouds writhe in their own metric tempo as veritable tissues of a thing alive.* —Guy Murchie

⋙ *From the moon, Earth is so small and so fragile, and such a precious little spot in that universe, that you can block it out with your thumb. Then you realize that on that spot, that little blue and white thing, is everything that means anything to you—all of history and music and poetry and art and death and birth and love, tears, joy, games, all of it right there on that little spot that you can cover with your thumb. And you realize from that perspective that you've changed forever, that there is something new there, that the relationship is no longer what it was.* —Rusty Schweickart, astronaut

⋙ *I viewed my mother quite differently when I was in the*

womb than I did after birth. Afterward, I was able to take more responsibility for her. —Rusty Schweickart

✒ *You say to yourself, "That's humanity, love, feeling, and thought." You don't see the barriers of color and religion and politics that divide this world. You wonder, if you could get everyone in the world up there, wouldn't they have a different feeling?* —Gene Cernan, astronaut

✒ *You only see the boundaries of nature from there, boundaries God created, not those that are manmade.* —Gene Cernan

✒ *You certainly come to the recognition that there aren't any political boundaries out there. You see it as one world, and you recognize how insignificant planet Earth is when you look at ten billion stars in the Milky Way and recognize that our sun is a rather minor one. You look out there millions of light years, and it is impossible to comprehend the vastness of space. It is humbling....I have always believed that there were other human beings on other planets. Not in our solar system, obviously, but I personally believe that God created our Earth and the universe and that we are not the only children of God in the universe.*
—Senator Edwin Garn of Utah, astronaut

✒ *Seeing Earth from a distance has changed my perception of the solar system as well. Ever since Copernicus's theory gained wide acceptance, people have considered it an irrefutable truth; yet I submit that we still cling emotionally to the pre-Copernican, or Ptolemaic, notion that Earth is the center of everything.* —Michael Collins, astronaut

✒ *I think the view from 100,000 miles could be invaluable in getting people to work out joint solutions, by causing them to realize that the planet we share unites us in a way far more ba-*

sic and far more important than differences in skin color or religion or economic system. The pity of it is that so far the view from 100,000 miles has been the exclusive property of a handful of test pilots, rather than the world leaders who need this new perspective, or poets who might communicate it to them. The best crew for an Apollo mission would be a philosopher, a priest, and a poet. Unfortunately, they would kill themselves trying to fly the spacecraft. —Michael Collins

⁂ *You recognize that the Russians, the Nicaraguans, the Canadians, the Filipinos—it doesn't matter where they're from—all they want to do is raise their kids and educate them, just as we do.* —Senator Edwin Garn

⁂ *I think the minute I saw the view for the first time was one of the most memorable moments of my entire life. I just said, in Arabic, "Oh, God," or something like "God is great!" when I saw the view. It was beyond description.*
—Sultan bin Salman al-Saud

⁂ *Earth... is a sparkling blue and white jewel...laced with slowly swirling veils of white...like a small pearl in a thick sea of black mystery.* —Edgar D. Mitchell, astronaut

⁂ *My view of our planet was a glimpse of divinity.*
—Edgar D. Mitchell

⁂ *Do I not fill heaven and earth? says the Lord.*
—Jeremiah 23:24

⁂ *When I was the last man to walk on the moon in December 1972, I stood in the blue darkness and looked in awe at Earth from the lunar surface. What I saw was almost too beautiful to grasp. There was too much logic, too much purpose—it was just too beautiful to have happened by accident. It doesn't matter how you choose to worship God....God has to exist to have created what I was privileged to see.* —Gene Cernan

❧ *Earth is a Paradise, the only one we will ever know. We realize it the moment we open our eyes. We don't have to make it a Paradise—it is one. We have only to make ourselves fit to inhabit it.* —Henry Miller

❧ *Viewed from the moon, the most astonishing thing about Earth is that it is alive....Beneath the moist, gleaming membrane of bright blue sky, it has the self-contained look of a live creature full of information, marvelously skilled in handling the sun.* —Lewis Thomas

❧ *Ask the animals, and they shall teach you; the birds of the air, and they shall instruct you. Speak to Earth and it shall teach you.* —Job 12:7–8

❧ *On the return trip home, gazing toward the stars and the planet from which I had come, I suddenly experienced the universe as intelligent, loving, harmonious.* —Edgar D. Mitchell

❧ *The Pythagoreans held the cosmos to be spherical, animate, ensouled, and intelligent.* —J. Donald Hughes

❧ *The peaks were the recognition that it is a harmonious, purposeful, creating universe. The valleys came in recognizing that humanity wasn't behaving in accordance with that knowledge.* —Edgar D. Mitchell

❧ *Earth is an organic spaceship. It lives.* —Noel McInnes

❧ *It is a peculiar fact that all the great astronomers of the 15th and 16th centuries were deeply convinced that the whole universe was a huge living being. Even during the height of western culture, the Greeks thought of the Living Planet organism as a fact of life.* —Eugene Kolisco

ᐤ Our bodies are not distinct from Earth, sun, moon, and other heavenly bodies. —Wendell Berry

ᐤ On the way back from the moon, while contemplating Earth, Edgar Mitchell had a "peak experience or religious experience." It was an "explosion of awareness, an aha! a wow!" It was, apparently, what a religious person would call a revelation. He came to realize that the universe is made up of spirit and matter but that they are not separate. The bridge is consciousness. God is something like a universal consciousness manifest in each individual, and the route to divine reality and to a more satisfying human, material reality is through human consciousness. —Omni, May 1984

ᐤ One's real, most intimate self pervades the universe and all other beings. The mountains, the sea, and the stars are part of one's body. —Willis Harmon

ᐤ This is us, Earth. We realize it sooner or later, but there is no getting around it. If we do not learn to live in harmony with the food chains, with the ecosystems, then gradually they will come out of balance, and then they will die. It is all a circle/cycle and we are in it; we cannot escape. —Baden Powell

ᐤ I characterize spaceflight as the metaphor for the technology of the twentieth century, during which science and technology have exploded. The unfortunate thing is that our morals are still rooted in the thirteenth or fourteenth century. Spaceflight, getting outside of Earth and seeing it from a different perspec-

tive, having this sort of explosive awareness that some of us had, this abiding concern and passion for the well-being of Earth—a more universal point of view—will have a direct impact on philosophy and value systems....It is precisely this shift in viewpoint and what it implies for the capacity of the human being and for our view of the universe that makes it so powerful. —Edgar D. Mitchell

❧ *The clear message of seeing ourself from space is that Earth is a whole system and humanity one of its many interdependent species. A regard for all of life as sacred becomes a practical as well as moral position when we see the critical role that all life plays in maintaining the system....If the next step in human evolution is to build a planetary civilization, then what is most needed is the ability to see and deal with problems and opportunities on a planetary level. It is also the ability not only to observe, but to truly communicate with, the planet as a whole. This message is implicit in the whole Earth symbol itself....To millions of Christians all over the planet, the cross is a symbol of unity in spite of deep divisions of race, language, and political beliefs. Because symbols work at a subconscious level, often unnoticed by the conscious mind, it makes sense that this new symbol might be having a quiet, though dramatic effect as a unifying force, too.* —Frank White

❧ *With all the arguments, pro and con, for going to the moon, no one suggested that we should do it to look at Earth. But that may in fact have been the most important reason of all.* —Joseph P. Allen, astronaut

❧ **"...for in God we live and move and have our being."** —Paul (Acts 17:28)

Questions for Reflection and Discussion

1. What were your favorite quotes in this chapter? Why?

2. What did you find most exciting in this chapter? Most challenging? Most insightful? Most disturbing? Why?

3. Was there anything in Chapter 5 about which you might say, "At some level I think that I have always known this. I've just never thought about it like that or put it in those words"? If so, what was it?

4. In addition to the suggestions that the author makes, what are some other ways to begin to develop the habit of "being the planet"?

5. If you were to intentionally memorize or internalize three of the meditations/affirmations over the next month, which three would you choose? Why? What method(s) might you use to help ensure that they become deeply ingrained within you?

6. If you were to write out and then internalize two or more of your own meditations/affirmations for life, what would they be?

7. When you close your eyes and imagine your relationship with God and creation, what do you see, hear, and feel?

8. What are some of the common themes that run through the quotes in the section, "Earth Looks in the Mirror"?

❧ 6 ❧

Resources

Andruss, Van, Christopher Plant, *et. al. Home! A Bioregional Reader*. Philadelphia: New Society Publishers, 1990. A collection of ideas and possibilities offered by an outstanding group of bioregional thinkers and activists. This book presents a realistic vision and strategy for creating ecologically sustainable communities and cultures in harmony with the limits and regenerative powers of the Earth. Highly recommended.

Avery, Michael, *et. al. Building United Judgment: A Handbook for Consensus Decision Making*. Madison, Wisc.: The Center for Conflict Resolution, 1981. Describes the attitudes, techniques, and skills that groups can apply to maximize cooperation and participation of all group members. Considered to be one of the best books on the subject.

Bartusiak, Marcia. *Thursday's Universe: A Report from the Frontier on the Origin, Nature, and Destiny of the Universe*. Redmond, Wash.: Tempus Books, 1988 (revised). A lucid presentation of recent developments in astronomy and cosmology. The *New York Times* cited this book as one of the best science books of 1987, and the Astronomical Society of the Pacific named it a 1987 Astronomy Book of the Year.

Bateson, Gregory. *Steps to an Ecology of Mind*. New York: Ballantine Books, 1972. *Mind and Nature: A Necessary Unity*.

New York: Bantam Books, 1980. Bateson shows how we must think if we are to be reconciled to our true nature—how to "think as nature thinks," and regain our place in the natural world. Weighty reading, but well worth the effort.

Berry, Thomas. *Befriending the Earth.* Mystic, Conn.: Twenty-Third Publications, 1991. This 13-part video series (a set of dialogues between Passionist priest, scholar, and geologian Thomas Berry and Jesuit priest and theologian Thomas Clarke) is an exploration of Berry's theology of reconciliation between humans and Earth. An excellent introduction to the thought of one of this century's most significant thinkers. Highly recommended.

Berry, Thomas. *Befriending the Earth: A Theology of Reconciliation Between Humans and the Earth.* Mystic, Conn.: Twenty-Third Publications, 1991. A book based on the video series, containing much of the dialogue with theologian Thomas Clarke.

Berry, Thomas. *The Dream of the Earth.* San Francisco: Sierra Club Books, 1988. An enlightening and empowering presentation of our modern cosmology. Berry explores the implications of our new creation story with regard to energy, technology, ecology, economics, education, spirituality, patriarchy, bioregionalism, Christianity, and more. He also includes a helpful annotated bibliography. Donald Conroy, President of the North American Conference on Religion and Ecology, recently stated, "This volume quite possibly is one of the ten most important books of the twentieth century."

Berry, Thomas, and Brian Swimme. *The Universe Story: An Autobiography of Planet Earth.* New York: Harper & Row, 1992. A most significant work. Wonderful reading. Highly recommended.

Berry, Wendell. *The Unsettling of America: Culture and Agriculture.* New York: Sierra Club Books, 1978. *Home Economics.* San Francisco: North Point Press, 1987. *Remembering.* San Francisco: North Point Press, 1988. Berry develops the theme of the interdependence of humans and the land in many ways. The first book is a classic. In the second, the essay "Two Economies" concerns the kingdom of God, and is worth the price of the book by itself. The third is the latest addition to a series of excellent short novels by Berry.

Birch, Charles. *A Purpose for Everything: Religion in a Postmodern World.* Mystic, Conn.: Twenty-Third Publications, 1990. An introductory and non-technical account of process thought written by a philosopher and biologist. Birch explores how the world is made up not of random bits and pieces, but of purposeful events and processes.

Bowman, Douglas C. *Beyond the Modern Mind: The Spiritual and Ethical Challenge of the Environmental Crisis.* New York: Pilgrim Press, 1990. Written by a professor of religion and Presbyterian minister, this book is about the shift in thinking that is required if our children will "inherit the Earth."

Briggs, John, and F. David Peat. *Looking Glass Universe: The Emerging Science of Wholeness.* New York: Simon & Schuster, 1984. *Turbulent Mirror: An Illustrated Guide to Chaos Theory and the Science of Wholeness.* New York: Harper & Row, 1989. These books are both excellently written and illustrated, and each is an exciting introduction to the cutting edge of scientific thought.

Brown, Lester R., *et. al. State of the World 1991: A Worldwatch Institute Report.* New York: W.W. Norton, 1991. Since 1984 the Worldwatch Institute has published this comprehensive annual report of Earth's condition. Using a broad range of informational sources, the report monitors changes in land, water, energy, and biological systems. For a sobering look at the present health of our larger body, Earth, this is probably the most accurate reference available.

Brown, Tom, Jr. *The Vision*. New York: Berkley Books, 1988. Brown, who trained for ten years with an Apache shaman and scout, writes this moving presentation of Native American wisdom and spiritual depth. His teacher, Stalking Wolf, is a beautiful example of Christ-likeness. Brown has written a number of books and field guides, all of which are informative, empowering, and eminently readable.

Caduto, Michael J., and Joseph Bruchac. *Keepers of the Earth: Native American Stories and Environmental Activities for Children*. Golden, Col.: Fulcrum, Inc., 1988. An excellent resource for parents and teachers.

Campbell, Joseph, with Bill Moyers. *The Power of Myth*. New York: Doubleday, 1988. The transcripts of the widely acclaimed PBS television series by the same name in which Bill Moyers interviewed Joseph Campbell over several months just prior to Campbell's death in 1987. A wonderful summing up of the work of one of the greatest mythologists of our time.

Capra, Fritjof. *The Turning Point: Science, Society, and the Rising Culture*. New York: Bantam Books, 1983. An exciting look at how discoveries in the sciences over the last century are beginning to usher in a whole new way of being human. Capra, a physicist, chronicles how we have reached a time of dramatic change, a turning point for the planet as a whole.

Cohen, Michael J. *How Nature Works: Regenerating Kinship with Planet Earth.* Walpole, N.H.: Stillpoint Publishing, 1988. *Connecting With Nature.* Eugene, Or.: World Peace University, 1989. These are both empowering and practical guides to living in a close personal relationship with the living Earth.

Cornell, Joseph Bharat. *Sharing Nature With Children.* Ananda Publications, 1979. *Sharing the Joy of Nature.* Nevada City, Cal.: Dawn Publications, 1989. Widely considered to be two of the best resources available for nature-awareness activities for children of all ages (including adults).

Creation. Friends of Creation Spirituality, Inc., 160 E. Virginia St., #290, San Jose, CA 95112. A high-quality, bimonthly periodical that deals with all aspects of creation spirituality. Matthew Fox is the editor-in-chief.

Eiseley, Loren. *The Immense Journey.* New York: Random House, 1960. *The Unexpected Universe.* New York: Harcourt Brace Jovanovich, 1972. *The Star Thrower.* New York: Times Books, 1978. Eisely is an anthropologist, naturalist, and gifted writer. Thomas Berry has said that he is "one of our most impressive thinkers on the human situation within the rhythms and mystique of Earth."

Ford, Adam. *Universe: God, Science, and the Human Person.* Mystic, Conn.: Twenty-Third Publications, 1987. This book addresses from a Christian perspective some of the more interesting problems posed by the science-religion dialogue. Includes helpful questions for reflection or discussion for each chapter.

Fox, Matthew. *The Coming of the Cosmic Christ.* San Francisco: Harper & Row, 1988. *Original Blessing: A Primer in Creation*

Spirituality. Santa Fe: Bear & Company, 1983. Fox was one of the first to explore the riches of the Christian tradition in light of the new cosmology. He breaks a lot of new ground. His books are also chock-full of quotes on creation spirituality themes from a wide variety of authors.

Fox, Warwick. *Toward a Transpersonal Ecology: Developing New Foundations for Environmentalism*. Boston: Shambhala Publications, 1990. This is an invaluable book on deep ecology. As Bill Devall notes, "It is an excellent book that will be used as a benchmark for all discussions of environmental philosophy in the 1990s." No doubt.

Gonick, Larry. *The Cartoon History of the Universe, Volumes 1-7: From the Big Bang to Alexander the Great*. New York: Doubleday, 1990. A real treat!

In Context: A Quarterly of Sustainable Culture. Context Institute, P.O. Box 11470, Bainbridge Island, WA 98110. Subscriptions are $18 per year and back issues are $5 each (and worth every penny). A first-rate journal about thinking and living in harmony with nature. Highly recommended.

Jantsch, Erich. *The Self-Organizing Universe: Scientific and Human Implications of the Emerging Paradigm of Evolution*. New York: Pergamon Press, 1980. This significant work examines the inner dynamism of the universe from its origin through the development of humanity. By "self-organizing" Jantsch is refering to the fact that the entire universe, at all levels, can be understood as an organic, developing whole.

Joseph, Lawrence E. *Gaia: The Growth of an Idea*. New York: St. Martin's Press, 1990. A helpful overview of the scientific debate about the Gaia hypothesis over the past decade.

Kelly, Kevin W. (for the Association of Space Explorers.) *The Home Planet*. New York: Addison Wesley, 1988. A large, beautiful book of breathtaking photos of the Earth from space, juxtaposed with quotes from American and Soviet astronauts.

Keyes, Ken, Jr. *Handbook to Higher Consciousness*. Coos Bay, Or.: Living Love Publications, 1975. An easy-to-read guide to growing in love, compassion, acceptance, and spiritual consciousness. Several of the "meditations/affirmations for life" in our Chapter 5 draw their inspiration from this fine book.

LaChance, Albert. *Greenspirit: The Twelve Steps of Green Spirituality*. New York: Element Books, 1991. A timely and practical guide to withdrawing from addictive consumerism and living a profoundly "down to earth" lifestyle. This book is a synthesis of the new cosmology and a twelve-step recovery process. It is highly recommended. LaChance has also written a powerful (though not yet published) 1500-line prophetic poem entitled *Jonah*.

Lonergan, Anne, and Caroline Richards, ed. *Thomas Berry and the New Cosmology*. Mystic, Conn.: Twenty-Third Publications, 1987. An appreciative yet critical examination of Berry's interpretation of the new cosmology by a wide range of Christian scholars. It contains a helpful bibliography.

Lovelock, James E. *The Ages of Gaia: A Biography of Our Living Earth*. New York: W.W. Norton, 1988. Includes the latest findings of scientists concerning Earth as an evolving, living being. The evidence is compelling.

MacGillis, Miriam Therese. "Earth Learning and Spirituality" (5-hour videotape) and "The Fate of the Earth" (90-minute audiotape). Global Perspectives, P.O. Box 925, Sonoma, CA 95476, (707) 996-4704. These tapes have significantly shaped my own thinking and are very highly recommended. Sr. Miriam is an exceptionally effective communicator of the new cosmology. Other tapes of hers (as well as of Berry and Swimme) are also available through Global Perspectives. Write for a listing at the address above.

Margulis, Lynn, and Dorian Sagan. *Micro-cosmos: Four Billion Years of Microbial Evolution*. New York: Summit Books, 1986. Margulis is co-author with James Lovelock of the Gaia theory. This book is a fascinating look at the invisible (to the naked eye) world of life and its role in the evolution of our living planet. You will never think of bacteria in the same way again! The authors argue convincingly for the primacy of cooperation over competition in the evolution of life. See also Margulis. *Early Life*. Boston: Science Books International, 1982, and Margulis and Karlene V. Schwartz. *Five Kingdoms: An Illustrated Guide to the Phyla of Life on Earth*. San Francisco: Freeman, 1982.

Marshall, Gene and Joyce. *The Reign of Reality*. Realistic Living Press, 1987. *A Primer on Radical Christianity*. Realistic Living Press, 1985. P.O. Box 140826, Dallas TX 75214 (214) 324-4629. The Marshalls present a down-to-earth form of prophetic religion that seems destined to be the direction Christianity will head in the third millenium. They have developed an "Expanding Notebook for House Church Co-Pastors," a valuable resource, as is their *Realistic Living Journal*. All of their material is highly recommended.

McDaniel, Jay. *Earth, Sky, Gods & Mortals: Developing an Ecological Spirituality*. Mystic, Conn.: Twenty-Third Publications, 1990. Thomas Berry writes the foreword to this fine synthesis of traditional and contemporary wisdom that points in the direction of an ecologically sound and nurturing faith. Helpful bibliography.

McDonagh, Sean. *To Care for the Earth: A Call to a New Theology.* Santa Fe: Bear & Company, 1987. McDonagh, an Irish Columban missionary who has worked in the Philippines for many years, writes this passionate appeal for a theology built on the new scientific/spiritual story of creation. This is a wide-ranging and insightful work.

McFague, Sallie. *Models of God: Theology for an Ecological, Nuclear Age.* Philadelphia: Fortress Press, 1987. McFague first examines the metaphorical nature of all theology. She then offers "the world as God's body" as a primary metaphor for God's relationship to creation, and suggests the biblical legitimacy and fruitfulness of relating to God, in addition to traditional ways, as Mother, Lover, and Friend. A most important theological work.

McGaa, Ed, Eagle Man. *Mother Earth Spirituality: Native American Paths to Healing Ourselves and Our World.* New York: Harper & Row, 1990. An introduction to Native American philosophy, history, and rituals, written by an Oglala Sioux lawyer who knows the Native path and can communicate the beauty and power of that path with excellence.

Murchie, Guy. *The Seven Mysteries of Life: An Exploration of Science and Philosophy.* Boston: Houghton Mifflin Company, 1978. A near comprehensive and fascinating exploration of life.

Neihardt, John G. *Black Elk Speaks: Being the Life Story of a Holy Man of the Oglala Sioux.* Lincoln, Neb.: University of Nebraska Press, 1961. One of the most important spiritual autogiographies of the twentieth century. Highly recommended.

Ong, Walter J. *Orality and Literacy: The Technologizing of the Word.* New York: Routledge, Chapman, and Hall, 1985. This important book explores some of the profound shifts in our consciousness, personality, spirituality, and social structures which are a result of the development of speech, writing, and print. Ong also projects his analysis into the age of mass electronic communications media. As Robert Giddings put it, "The cumulative impact of this book is dazzling."

Ornstein, Robert, and Paul Ehrlich. *New World, New Mind.* New York: Simon & Schuster, 1989. An important look at how we must have an evolution of consciousness, that is, how we must learn to perceive and think differently if we are to avoid ecological catastrophe.

Peck, M. Scott. *The Different Drum: Community Making and Peace.* New York: Simon & Schuster, 1987. An insightful and empowering look at the nature of true community at all levels of society. Peck offers practical suggestions on how community can be established and maintained in order that the world might be saved.

Plant, Christopher, and Judith Plant. *Turtle Talk: Voices for a Sustainable Future.* Philadelphia: New Society Publishers, 1990. A series of engaging and inspiring interviews with bioregionally oriented activists, visionaries, organizers, and poets—all of whom share their passion for Earth, for human communities, and for creative change.

Porritt, Jonathan. *Seeing Green: The Politics of Ecology Explained.* New York: Basil Blackwell, 1984. On developing an ecological approach to reality, particularly in the political and economic spheres.

Rifkin, Jeremy, ed. *The Green Lifestyle Handbook*. New York: Henry Holt & Co., 1990. A comprehensive guide to developing a wholly "green" lifestyle, written by twenty-three leading environmental and ecological thinkers.

Robbins, John. *Diet for a New America*. Walpole, N.H.: Stillpoint Publishing, 1987. This book has the potential of awakening the conscience of our nation in much the way that Rachel Carson's *Silent Spring* did in the 1960s. It is about how our food choices affect our health, happiness, and the future of life on Earth. An important and readable work. Highly recommended.

Sagan, Carl. *Cosmos*. New York: Ballantine Books, 1985. This is the bestselling science book ever published, and for good reason. It is an excellent introduction to science as a whole and a fascinating journey through the wonders and mysteries of the universe. The book is based on the thirteen part Emmy and Peabody award-winning PBS television series by the same name.

Sahtouris, Elisabet. *Gaia: The Human Journey from Chaos to Cosmos*. New York: Pocket Books, 1989. A persuasive, easy to read, and wonderful telling of our cosmic evolutionary story. It is perhaps the best book available on the Gaia theory. Very highly recommended. She has also written a simplified version of the story for young adults entitled, *Gaia's Dance*. It, too, is wonderful, though not yet published.

Sale, Kirkpatrick. *Dwellers in the Land: The Bioregional Vision*. San Francisco: Sierra Club Books, 1985. This is perhaps the best introduction to bioregional philosophy and practice available at the present time. Highly recommended.

Sale, Kirkpatrick. *The Conquest of Paradise: Christopher Columbus and the Columbian Legacy*. New York: Alfred A. Knopf, 1990. Cuts through the myths that have built up around the "discovery of America." As Bill McKibben says, "In his impressive book, Kirkpatrick Sale shows that the first voyages of 'discovery' offer little for us to celebrate. This is not inspiring history, but it is absolutely necessary history; for the sad patterns set in 1492 govern our relationship with the New World to this day. Perhaps the five-hundredth anniversary will begin a new truth-telling. If so, this book will have been an important cause."

Schindler, Craig, and Gary Lapid. *The Great Turning: Personal Peace, Global Victory*. Santa Fe: Bear & Company, 1989. This is a book on how we must think, plan, cooperate, communicate, and transform conflict if are to survive the present global crisis and mature as a human family.

Schumacher, E. F. *Small Is Beautiful: Economics as If People Mattered*. New York: Harper & Row, 1975. Clearly shows the absurdity and the long-term consequences of the growth obsession that has dominated our industrial economy. It offers a realistic, though radical, vision of economics and technology scaled down to a sustainable size. A classic.

Seed, John, Joanna Macy, *et. al. Thinking Like a Mountain: Toward a Council of All Beings*. Philadelphia: New Society Publishers, 1988. This collection of essays, group exercises, and poetry is a valuable aid to personally experiencing the revelation that we are each like cells within a living planet which is our larger Self. Highly recommended.

Sheldrake, Rupert. *The Presence of the Past: Morphic Resonance and the Habits of Nature*. New York: Random House Times Books, 1988. This suberb book challenges most of the fundamental assumptions of a mechanistic understanding of the universe. Sheldrake supports his hypothesis that nature at every level has memory. Another example of the move of modern science away from reductionism and toward a more organic and wholistic understanding of reality.

Swimme, Brian. *The Universe Is a Green Dragon: A Cosmic Creation Story*. Santa Fe: Bear & Company, 1984. Written by a physicist who has studied extensively with Thomas Berry, this book is a gem. It is an alluring introduction to the new cosmology, an adventure into the basic dynamics of the cosmos. It deserves to be read more than once.

Swimme, Brian. "Canticle to the Cosmos." Tides Foundation, NewStory Project, 134 Coleen St., Livermore, CA 94550. This twelve-part video lecture series tells the story of the universe with a feeling for its sacred nature. Designed to be used as part of an academic curriculum, in small group study, or for personal enrichment, each presentation is one hour in length and is complete in itself. This is a wonderful, very highly recommended series.

Teilhard de Chardin, Pierre. *The Phenomenon of Man*. New York: Harper & Row, 1959. Teilhard, a professional geologist, paleontologist, is considered to be the grandfather of the new cosmology. This presentation of the story of the universe, completed in its first version in 1940, was the earliest scientific account of the universe as a spiritual as well as material process. This book is a Christ-centered, scientific classic. See also his *Christianity and Evolution*. San Diego: Harcourt Brace Jovanovich, 1969.

Thomas, Lewis. *The Lives of a Cell: Notes of a Biology Watcher.* New York: Bantam, 1975. This is a well written collection of essays by a widely respected biologist. Thomas suggests that the most accurate way of seeing Earth is as one majestic cell, with all forms of life as organelles within the larger cell.

Thompson, William Irwin, ed. *Gaia: A Way of Knowing.* Great Barrington, Mass.: Lindisfarne Press, 1987. A series of essays by significant thinkers dealing with the political implications of the new biology.

Turner, Frederick. *Beyond Geography: The Western Spirit Against the Wilderness.* New Brunswick, N.J.: Rutgers University Press, 1983. A remarkable and disturbing account of Western civilization and its pervasive antagonism toward the natural world and native cultures. Written in a splendid prose style.

Van Matre, Steve. *Earth Education.* Warrenville: The Institute for Earth Education,1990. *The Earth Speaks.* Warrenville: IEE, 1983. These are both rich resources for nature education and Earth learning. Every teacher should own the first. The second is a collection of passages from a wide variety of nature writers.

Watson, Lyall. *Lifetide: The Biology of the Unconscious.* New York: Simon and Schuster, 1979. A fascinating examination of the universe and our role within it.

White, Frank. *The Overview Effect.* Boston: Houghton Mifflin Company, 1987. This is a book about the transforming effect that seeing the planet from space has had on the majority of astronauts and cosmonauts. It is also about how their experiences are helping to facilitate a worldwide shift in perspective, an evolution of human consciousness. Many of the quotes in the last section were gathered from this book.

Zinn, Howard. *A People's History of the United States*. New York: Harper & Row, 1980. This book is unsettling to say the least. It is a look at the history of our country not from the perspective of the rich and powerful white, male leadership, but from the perspective of women, minorities, the oppressed, and those who lived here for tens of thousands of years before Columbus arrived. Chapter 1, "Columbus, the Indians, and Human Progress," documents from sources including Columbus's personal journal the brutality inflicted by him on the Arawak Indians of the Bahamas, who were a peaceful people. It goes on to document how what Columbus did to the Arawaks, Cortes did to the Azteca of Mexico, Pizarro did to the Incas of Peru, and the English settlers of Virginia and Massachusetts did to the Powhatans and the Pequots. That chapter alone is worth the price of the book. For all who want a more complete picture of the history of our country than is usually taught in school, this book is a must.

Questions for Reflection and Discussion

1. What are the 3 to 5 books or authors that seem potentially most interesting to you at this time in your life? Why?

2. If you were to start a long-term, self-directed course of study in the new cosmology with this resource list as a guide, where would you begin? What would your approach be? Why?

Pledge of Allegiance to the Earth

I pledge allegiance to the Earth
for the sake of all its future plant,
animal, and human forms of life.
One living planet
revealing God;
wholly lovable,
with clean air, water, and soil,
liberty and justice for all.

Do you find this pledge of allegiance helpful? If so, what are some ways that you might introduce it into your community? If not, what changes would you make?

Michael Dowd is presently serving as pastor of St. Paul's United Church of Christ in Woodsfield, Ohio. His interests and involvements are in storytelling, ecological peace and justice, nonviolence, community life and development, camping, backpacking, Native American life and spirituality, holistic health and well-being, the twelve-step recovery process, small groups, gardening, bioregionalism, family spirituality and rituals (i.e., sacramental living), and home education. He loves to read, and when he has the time enjoys playing chess, basketball, table tennis, racketball, softball, and golf. Michael and his wife, Alison (a storyteller, gifted singer, and educator) have three children: Sheena, 8; Shane, 6; and Miriam Joy, an infant.

Michael is available to speak with both church and non-church groups, guide independent studies, and lead workshops or retreats in the new cosmology, ecological theology, or creation spirituality. He and Alison also do storytelling together for both children and adults. For more information please write or call: Michael and Alison Dowd, 307 South Main Street, Woodsfield, OH 43793. (614) 472-0365